An Anthology of
EARLY
RENAISSANCE
MUSIC

Also edited by Noah Greenberg:

An Anthology of English Medieval and Renaissance Vocal Music

With W. H. Auden and Chester Kallman:
An Anthology of Elizabethan Lute Songs, Madrigals, and Rounds

An Anthology of
EARLY RENAISSANCE MUSIC ∾

Edited by

Noah Greenberg
AND
Paul Maynard

W·W·NORTON & COMPANY·INC· New York

Copyright © 1975 by W. W. Norton & Company, Inc.

First Edition

All Rights Reserved

Published simultaneously in Canada
by George J. McLeod Limited, Toronto

Library of Congress Cataloging in Publication Data
Main entry under title:
An Anthology of early Renaissance music.

Bibliography: p.
Includes index.
1. Instrumental music—To 1800. 2. Vocal music—To 1800. 3. Music—History
and criticism—Medieval, 400–1500. 4. Music—History and criticism—16th century.
I. Greenberg, Noah. II. Maynard, Paul.
M2.A517   780'.903'1   75–11747
ISBN 0–393–02182–3

Printed in the United States of America

1 2 3 4 5 6 7 8 9 0

Acknowledgments

The following music selections and plates have been supplied by the owners or custodians, whose courtesy is gratefully acknowledged:

Nos. 1 and 8: American Institute of Musicology, Dr. Armen Carapetyan, director

No. 2: American Musicological Society

Nos. 3, 4, 11, 13, 22, and 30: editions of Vereiniging voor Nederlandse Muziekgeschiedenis Alsbach & Co.

No. 5: The University of Michigan Press

Chants for Nos. 5, 6, 9, 10, and 12: Desclée & Cie, éditeurs

Nos. 6, 19, 24: Möseler Verlag

No. 7: The Royal Musical Association

Nos. 9 and 28: Bärenreiter-Verlag

No. 15: Éditions de L'Oiseau-Lyre

No. 21: Librairie Droz S.A.

Nos. 26 and 40: Istituto Español de Musicologia

No. 27: Curtis Brown, Ltd.

No. 29: G. Schirmer, Inc.

Nos. 31 and 32: The Medieval Academy of America

No. 34: Wilhelm Hansen, Musik-Forlag

No. 39: Martinus Nijhoff's Boekhanden en Uitgeversmaatschappij B.V.

Plate 1: Museum of Fine Arts, Boston, Massachusetts

Plate 2: Biblioteca Capitular y Colombina, Seville

Plate 4: Gesellschaft der Freunde der Albertina, Vienna

Plates 5, 10, and 12: Fratelli Alinari, Florence

Plate 6: Harvard College Library

Plate 7: Rare Book Division, The New York Public Library, Astor, Lenox and Tilden Foundations

Plate 8: The British Library Board, London

Plate 9: The Newberry Library, Chicago, Illinois

Plate 11: The Pierpont Morgan Library, New York

Plate 13: The John Carter Brown Library, Brown University, Providence, Rhode Island

Music examples on p. 315 from G. Reese, *Music in the Renaissance*, rev. ed. (New York, 1959), pp. 44–45.

Contents

Illustrations follow p. 146

Foreword

When I recently cast my eyes over the Table of Contents of this collection, one of my first reactions was pleasure at recognizing many old friends whose worth has become ever more evident the longer I have known them. Close upon this recognition came the realization that many of the compositions had become warm, living companions largely as a result of the revitalizing work of Noah Greenberg. However alluring this or that work of the Middle Ages or Renaissance might have looked on paper, it was, of course, the actual sound that could and did arouse a really hearty response; and, when Noah launched his New York Pro Musica concerts in 1952, he gave a freshness and richness to the performance of early music that contributed immensely to the revival that had for some time been gathering momentum. Certainly his performances—with their rewards for the trained scholar as well as the inquiring student, for the intelligent performer as well as the concertgoer and record collector—came at a time when, at least in the United States, there was an urgent need for a group of professional executants to convert, into fully artistic sound, some of the ever-increasing repertory that the international body of scholars had been turning into generally comprehensible notation. Noah and his brave band established a standard of performance for their countrymen, and they were appreciated abroad. The standard has made history. Every *collegium musicum* in this country that performs early music (and this includes virtually all of them) is in a way an outgrowth of the New York Pro Musica. And, although Pro Musica itself no longer continues to function, some of its life continues to course through the veins of the excellent American professional organizations that specialize in early music. This was convincingly shown when, on September 29, 1974, no fewer than nine musical organizations and a dance group acknowledged their debt and rendered their homage by performing at a concert and Evensong in memory of Noah Greenberg at the Cathedral Church of St. John the Divine in New York.

This anthology gathers together a sampling of the repertory that Noah Greenberg helped make familiar over the years. It should serve as a guidebook, especially to *collegia musica,* but by no means only to them.

Paul Maynard, out of his· rich experience, sensitivity, and knowledge, has written comments on each piece, offering suggestions for performance. The eminent keyboard player of Pro Musica during much of its career as well as one of the distinguished conductors who succeeded Noah, he here functions not only as a living and authoritative voice of Pro Musica but as an independent, perceptive artist.

GUSTAVE REESE

Editor's Note

Before his untimely death in 1966, Noah Greenberg had made the final choice of pieces to be included in this book. My share has been the writing of the commentary and the Introduction. I am deeply grateful to a number of people for the help they so kindly gave me.

Many thanks must go to Professor Joel Newman of Columbia University for making the transcriptions of those pieces for which an original source was used. (These are indicated in each case by an asterisk placed before the source.) Professor Newman also supplied translations for the Latin texts of nos. 6, 11, 35, 36, and 40; for the Italian texts of nos. 24 and 25; and for the Spanish texts of nos. 26 and 39. He also lightened my research by sharing with me information that he had assembled on certain pieces.

Thanks go to Professor Paul R. Lonigan of Queens College of the City University of New York for his translations of the French texts of nos. 19, 20, 21, and 32; to Professor Dorothea Austin of Queensborough Community College of the City University of New York for her translations of the German texts of nos. 18 and 23; and to Professor Joseph Ponte of Queens College for the translations of nos. 15 and 36, and for valuable help in research matters.

I am warmly grateful to Professors Edward R. Lerner and Saul Novack, both of Queens College, for their help and advice on many points as well as for their personal encouragement. Professor Lerner kindly lent me his photostat of the *Graduale Pataviensi* (Basel, 1511), which contained the appropriate chant melody for Isaac's *Agnus Dei*.

I was fortunate in having Hinda Keller Farber, of W. W. Norton & Company, as editor of the manuscript. Working with her was truly a pleasure.

But the person to whom I owe the greatest debt of gratitude is my wife, Drora Pershing, lecturer in music at Queens College. Her extensive musical and historical background made her enormously helpful in much of the research that was necessary for the writing of the commentary. She also spent countless hours carefully and painstakingly revising what I had first written in order to make what I wanted to say clearer and more concise. Her support and encouragement were immeasurable. I will never be able to thank her enough, for this book would not have been the same without her.

In a broader sense, far beyond the bounds of this book, my greatest debt of all is to Noah Greenberg, with whom I had a long and happy association in the New York Pro Musica. The color, vitality, and depth of feeling in the performances of this ensemble were fired by his sound musical instinct, his vibrant imagination, and his loving understanding of the music.

PAUL MAYNARD

Bayside, New York
November, 1974

An Anthology of

EARLY
RENAISSANCE
MUSIC

Introduction

During the past several decades, the continuing work of many scholars throughout the world has lead to the publication of an enormous repertoire of Renaissance music in accurate, modern editions. In many cases, a Renaissance composer's entire surviving output is now available; in others, a "collected works" edition is in progress. There are also now available many extensive series, covering particular genres, specific countries, or the output of individual early printers. We are greatly indebted to generations of scholars for this immense work. Without it, the entire world of music, performer and listener alike, would have been immeasurably the poorer.

Because the original sources of Renaissance music contain no performance indications, we are faced by an enormous and agonizing gulf between the written notes and what might have been their realization in sound. Most of what little we do know about the performance of Renaissance music has been pieced together from several types of sources. The surviving earlier theoretical writings are often very vague and, in any case, contain only the most meager bits of information on performance. Firsthand accounts of specific performances, which often vividly convey the pomp and splendor of an important occasion or festivity, tell us at best only such things as what instruments were used or how many singers took part and how they were costumed, but nothing more detailed. Paintings and sculpture, surprisingly, can tell us more than we might expect, especially about suitable instrumental combinations. And finally, the instruments that have survived are themselves treasuries of information. For the most part, then, we have had to piece together unrelated bits of information from sources that were never intended for this purpose. As shaky as some of this information may be, the performer must seize upon it. Working painstakingly with early instruments (or good modern copies of them) and bringing into the fullest use the best of his general musical instinct and experience, he must carefully test out this information with loving patience and an open mind. For it is the performer, rather than the scholar, who must face all these questions head-on and try to find convincing solutions.

Unlike the practice of composers from more recent periods, Renaissance composers entrusted a great many elements of performance to the performer. To be sure, in many cases the composer himself prepared and directed the performance. But after the introduction of music printing by Petrucci in 1501, there was such a broad dissemination of music that there could be no possibility of the composer's presence at all the performances his music would now receive. We can only assume that—as with figured-bass realization and the art of ornamentation in the Baroque—performers were trained in a common tradition. Composers, themselves performers as well as teachers of many of the musicians, therefore saw no need to spell out either the more variable elements of performance, such as scoring, or the presumably less variable ones, such as *musica ficta* or text underlay. Thus we see that the Renaissance composer never thought of a single "correct" set of conditions for the performance of a given piece. On the contrary, it would have been totally foreign to him to think of his piece performed in only one, exactly specified way. Our goal, then, must be to use, to the best of our understanding, whatever information has been found about this unwritten performance tradition. Some of our questions may not be answered for another fifty years, and, almost certainly, still others will remain forever unanswered.

Why should we be so concerned about authenticity in performing Renaissance music? Surely there must be more reward than mere correctness for its own sake. One of the more extreme illustrations of this question is Handel's *Messiah,* which, until quite recently, was invariably performed with a chorus of 150 or 200 voices and a full symphony orchestra. The orchestral score, published by Ebenezer Prout in 1902, was a "realization" of Handel's score in terms of the late nineteenth-century symphonic idiom, complete with added wind and brass and even supplying orchestral versions of the keyboard realizations in the arias. Such an approach, naturally, steered conductors and soloists away from even the *thought* of ornamentation or cadenzas (for which Handel so clearly provided appropriate places). For years, Handel-Prout was held sacred, and not a note was omitted or altered. But, thanks to a great deal of information that has come to light in recent years about Baroque performance practice, *Messiah* has been transformed from that ponderous and solemn Victorian edifice into the sunny, thoughtful, moving, transparent, and captivating work that Handel originally created.

Many an organist has struggled desperately (though perhaps not quite knowing why) to play Bach's music on a huge, twentieth-century American organ. On such instruments (which are based on nineteenth-century concepts of organ design), the Romantic organ repertoire can sound marvelous, but Bach is often little more than intelligible, much less convincing. On the other hand, a Baroque-style organ (on which most of the Romantic organ literature is totally ineffective) will solve these problems, and a good Baroque organ will actually clarify the structure and interpretation of Bach's style for the organist.

These two examples serve to illustrate the point that unless the music of *any* period is re-created using approximately the performing machinery for which the composer wrote it, the performance has very little chance of fully communicating what the composer had to say. However, one must emphasize that no amount of "authenticity"—whether in *Messiah* or a Josquin Mass—can ever substitute for lack of technical polish in the performance. If, for some reason, such a substitution has to be made, it would be better for the "authentic" performance never to take place at all, because no information has yet come to light that would indicate that the best sixteenth-century singers and players were any less competent than their counterparts today.

Still, a general point remains: We know that we will almost certainly never be able to recreate fully the performances of past eras, especially as far back as the Renaissance. But suppose suddenly, by some miracle, we *could*. Now we hear the music just as the composer himself would have been pleased to hear it. Would such performances be completely meaningful for us today? Could we truly hear them as the Renaissance listener heard them, considering that all our lives we have also heard and studied Mozart, Wagner, and Stravinsky? Whether we like it or not, these experiences have a hidden effect on our under-

standing and interpretation of early music; and just as we have come to understand the different musical languages of Bach, Verdi, Debussy, and Bartók, so we must come to understand also the language of the Renaissance. We will find that none of these languages is intrinsically "better" or "worse" than the others, but only that each language is different, for, at bottom, they are all saying the same things. The late Thurston Dart expressed these thoughts so well in his *The Interpretation of Music:*

> The modern musician's approach to the music of his own time is obstructed by the past, and his approach to old music is through the gateway of the present. The figures most familiar to him are the composers of the last two centuries; the sonorities in use are those of the last fifty years, and they are the norm by which he judges the exotic and abnormal tone-colours of marimbas or novachords as well as the exotic and abnormal tone-colours of regals, viols or crumhorns. But to earlier musicians these tone-colours were the normal ones; concert grands, wire-strung violins and Boehm flutes would have been considered strange and abnormal.[1]

The scholar who has prepared the modern edition from which the performer is working has already coped with (at least to a workable degree) two of the many questions that confront the performer of Renaissance music. The first of these is the question of text underlay—that is, the precise, word-by-word fitting of text to notes, very often provided in the original sources only for one voice part, and not always even for that. The second is the question of *musica ficta*, the practice, unwritten by composers but well understood by Renaissance performers, of applying accidentals to certain notes. We will return to the second of these questions later. The questions that still remain for the performer to settle are tempo, scoring, dynamics, phrasing and articulation, ornamentation, performance pitch, and vocal quality.

TEMPO

In transcribing early Renaissance music into modern notation, most scholars, for the past several decades, have generally adopted the half note as the unit of one beat, except in Burgundian music, where a quarter-note unit has been

[1] T. Dart, *The Interpretation of Music*, Atlantic Highlands, N.J.: 1964, p. 164.

used instead. This practice has been followed in this book. However, it must be emphasized that in any modern edition the value chosen for the beat is purely arbitrary, whether it follows a commonly used convention or not, and that whatever note value is used has nothing to do with the tempo of the piece. (compare, for example, nos. 19 and 22). As in many cases of later music, one piece with a half-note beat may go faster than another with a quarter-note beat.

If the performer has not been misled into the disastrous notion that early and later music operate in fundamentally different ways, he will soon discover that tempos in Renaissance music are based on the same set of musical principles as in later music. Thus the tempo will depend partly on such factors as the shortest or longest notes occuring in a piece, the harmonic rhythm, and the general melodic style. And just as such features determine the whole character and mood of a work, the tempo, dictated by these same factors, will further reinforce this resulting character. Therefore, the tempo is inseparably bound up with such qualities of the piece as tenderness, playfulness, breadth, sadness, resignation, exuberance, or quiet joy.

It is these same qualities that will determine the strictness or freedom of the tempo. Fast, lively pieces, whether vigorous or light, need a strict tempo, and if the melodic and rhythmic elements of the music are handled properly, the strict tempo will never sound mechanical (see the comments under "Dynamics, Phrasing, and Articulation" below). A great many moderate or slow pieces need a steady but not strict tempo. Here the pulse should be gentle, so that there is room within the steady speed for those minute lengthenings and hastenings that allow the music to "breathe." But certain moderate-to-slow pieces that seem to be intimately personal expressions of tenderness, longing, fervor, sadness, or anguish require not only the minute freedoms just mentioned, but actual flexibility of the tempo itself (see nos. 10, 16, 18, 23b, and 36). With the exception of parts of no. 18, there is little or no imitative writing in these pieces; rather, they have either a homophonic or quasi-homophonic texture. This kind of texture makes a flexible tempo possible; the emotional qualities found in these pieces make it mandatory. On the other hand, Josquin's *Absalon fili mi,* though profoundly moving, cannot be performed with any significant tempo freedom because of the constantly interlocking imitative texture. And for the same reason, a flexible tempo is not needed and would, in fact, distort the piece if forced upon it.

Mention should be made here of proportional tempo relationships, found in so many works in Netherlands style. In these cases, one or more changes of time signature (mensural sign) occur during the course of the piece. (Bar lines did not come into use until the seventeenth century.) In all cases of a change of mensural sign, each new sign indicated not only the meter of each new section, but a tempo relationship as well. The simplest examples occur in duple-meter pieces that contain brief triple-meter passages. In all such cases, a measure of triple equals a measure of duple, making each beat in the triple section faster and generating a lighter, more rhythmic quality (see nos. 11, 12, 30, 38, 39, and 40). A more elaborate example occurs in Ockeghem's *Alma Redemptoris Mater.* Here, the successive mensural signs transcribe as $\frac{3}{2}$, $\mathbf{C}$, $\frac{6}{4}$, and $\frac{3}{2}$. As in the simpler cases just cited, the *length* of measure remains constant throughout this motet so that, in addition to the different metrical structure of each section, there will be a different speed of beat. All of these relationships work perfectly in performance.

Much more complicated proportional tempo relationships sometimes occur in movements that have several freestanding sections (see no. 4). In some cases of this type, the tempo relationships between the different sections can—and therefore should—be observed. ("Observed" need not necessarily mean a slavish and exact mathematical relationship. After all, listeners don't come to concert performances with pocket metronomes.) But in other cases, such relationships would be ludicrous in performance, since one tempo would be impossibly slow or another absurdly fast. In these instances, sizable compromises must be made, but the *general* relationships of tempo can still be preserved.

SCORING

Though surviving evidence indicates beyond any doubt that instruments played a crucial role in the performance of vocal music, little information is specific. As mentioned earlier, Renaissance composers gave no performance instructions in their manuscripts because the notion of a single, specified set of performance factors for a given piece would have been alien to their thinking. Rather, a piece was almost certainly performed differently on different occasions—in one instance taking advantage of especially good wind players, on another occasion substituting different instruments to suit a larger (or smaller) vocal group, at still another time reshaping a performance to please the personal preferences of a patron, or to make the piece especially effective for a particular entertainment or occasion of state, or to get the best results from the acoustics of a particular location. It is stretching the point too far to compare this kind of flexible approach to that of our own popular music of the last fifty years, yet some of that same flexibility is needed, for that is apparently how performance was approached in the Renaissance. No attempt can be made in this sort space to deal with the subject of scoring in any but the most general way. But it is hoped that this general approach, together with the specific performance suggestions given for each piece in this book, will provide the performer with practical principles that can then be applied to other pieces as well.

Instruments were used in the performance of vocal music in several ways: doubling the voices (in much of the sacred repertoire, which was intended for choral performance, but also in secular music) or taking the place of singers on one or more voice parts (sometimes in sacred music, but especially in the one-performer-to-a-part secular repertoire). In addition, an enormous number of vocal pieces were often performed entirely instrumentally—providing, in fact, a large part of the instrumentalists' repertoire. Certain compositions, however, seem unquestionably to have been intended for purely vocal performance.

Reinterpreting these points, we may state the following: (1) certain vocal pieces must have an *a cappella* performance; (2) many vocal works decidedly benefit from the inclusion of instruments; (3) some vocal works are equally successful either with or without instrumental doubling; (4) many vocal pieces (especially of the secular repertoire) readily lend themselves to a completely instrumental performance. Let us examine briefly the first two categories, primarily as they apply to choral performance.

One of the unique characteristics of the singing voice is the "yield" or "give" in its sound—an ephemeral quality instantly recognizable in the sound of a good choral ensemble, even in a resonant, perfectly supported *forte,* but especially in a sustained, slow-moving piece. Another exclusively vocal feature results from the fact that the text (regardless of the language) provides a rich and ever-changing combination of vocal colors mixed with a large vocabulary of attack and release sounds. Disregarding for the moment the whole question of text meanings, it is these ever-present word sounds, more than any other single element, that sets the world of vocal music apart from that of instrumental music. A third exceptional quality, partly related to the one just mentioned, is the voice's natural and effortless (perhaps one should say instinctive) ability to produce the most sensitive dynamic nuances. No instrument can fully duplicate these characteristics, and it is these features unique to the voice that are so essential for the performance of pieces of either unusual gentleness or warmth (see nos. 7, 10, 11, 18, and 23b) or intense emotion (see nos. 14 and 36). Certain fast pieces of a light or playful character need the agility that is typical of the singing voice (see nos. 15 and 24).

But a large number of choral pieces decidedly gain in performance by having instruments double the voices. The reasons can be summarized as follows: (1) Instruments provide a kind of solid, cohesive core for the vocal sound. (This solidifying of the vocal timbre is exactly what is *not* desirable in pieces best performed *a cappella*.) (2) In a polyphonic texture in which the voice parts lie close together, and especially in which the inner voices lie in exactly the same range and frequently cross, contrasting instrumental timbres help to distinguish the parts aurally. (3) In faster tempos, voices cannot give the quickest notes as much sound as the longer ones, especially when several quick notes are sung to the same syllable; yet the quick notes are vitally important to the rhythmic quality of the piece. These figures, performed *a cappella*, are likely to sound rather pallid, and in inner voices they may be lost altogether. Because they can play quick figures with the same loudness and clarity of articulation as longer notes, instruments doubling the voices help to make such details clear. (Again, the opposite condition is needed for a slower, expressive piece performed *a cappella*. There, the faster notes, which usually will not be particularly fast in any case, need the voice's natural tendency to sing them slightly more softly.) (4) The appropriate choice of instruments can enhance the general sonority (brightness, fullness, smoothness) desirable for the piece. (5) By playing in some sections of a piece, but not in others, instruments help to articulate the overall form of the piece (see nos. 1, 4, 12, 19, 38, and 39). (6) The mixed sound of voices and instruments together can give a greater sensuous pleasure than the sound of either group alone. (This factor is overruled in cases where *a cappella* performance is called for.)

Works for solo voice (most of the secular repertoire) must be approached in the same way as solo vocal music of any period—that is, the solo voice is meant to be heard alone on its own part, with its special vocal and musical characteristics undiluted by instrumental doubling or, for that matter, additional voices. But even here there can be no absolute rule to cover all cases. Some solo music can be equally effective performed instrumentally *instead* of vocally (see nos. 8, 19, 22, and 32), provided the instrumentalists are of solo caliber. On the other hand, in a work like Hayne's *Alles regretz* (no. 20), instrumental performance of the solo part (tenor) can probably never be adequate because of the many long notes; it is precisely this feature that requires the infinite flexibility of the singing voice.

Stylistic and structural aspects of a composition are determining factors in deciding questions of scoring. Here is a summary of the most commonly found situations:

In Burgundian pieces, the highest voice and the tenor usually have somewhat differing melodic characteristics, and, therefore, it is best for these parts to have contrasting timbres (either both parts sung by contrasting solo voices, or one part sung and the other played). The untexted contratenor part, thought by most present-day scholars to have been intended for an instrument, functions to a certain extent as a filling-in part, and should therefore have yet a third contrasting timbre. In this way, two musical requirements can be met: (1) the filling-in contratenor can be given slightly less weight than the tenor (when, for example, viol plays the tenor and lute the contratenor) and (2) the frequent voice crossings of these parts can be made clearer by their contrasting timbres. To summarize, Burgundian *a 3* pieces usually are most effectively performed with contrasting timbres for all three parts (see nos. 6, 8, 19, and 21).

Among the Burgundian pieces in our collection are two whose voice parts have far less melodic differentiation than usual: the anonymous

Die Katzen Pfote (no. 28) and Busnois's *Fortuna desperata* (no 29). These pieces can be performed equally well with either similar or contrasting timbres. And finally, an exception to the question of timbre contrast in Burgundian music is found in the Dufay Kyrie (no. 1). Here, because the three voice-parts have an essentially similar melodic style and move homorhythmically a good deal of the time, a basically similar timbre on all three parts is preferable.

Flemish music presents an entirely different situation from the more usual (timbre contrast) Burgundian music, for one of its fundamental characteristics (except for certain cases discussed below) is that all voice parts have equal importance and, in the majority of works, similar melodic content. Therefore, the general tendency should be to use similar rather than contrasting timbres. But again, this is not a hard-and-fast rule, and many Flemish pieces can be successfully performed with a scoring of mixed timbres, provided the parts are heard with equal balance.

Certain Flemish pieces, however, will actually benefit from timbre contrast. Among these are pieces containing canonic treatment. In Isaac's earlier version of *Innsbruck* (no. 23a) and Josquin's *Petite camusette* (no. 22), the respective song tunes are stated canonically in the inner voices. Since the two canonic voices are identical, they should have the same timbre, but the pair should be set off by contrasting timbres in the other voice parts. However, two cases in which a canon should *not* be differentiated from the other parts are Isaac's Agnus Dei (no. 5) and *Gaudeamus omnes* (no. 12, mm. 55–65). Here, in spite of the presence of canon, all four voice-parts are absolutely similar in melodic style and are woven together in the most sensitive and flexible kind of polyphonic texture. The special richness and expressiveness of such a texture is far more important than emphasis of the canon and can be largely destroyed if the canonic voices are in any significant way set apart from the others.

Pieces like Isaac's later setting of *Innsbruck* (no. 23b) or Encina's *Triste España sin ventura* (no. 26), both of which have the principal melody in the highest voice with the lower voices moving homophonically (in the Encina) or quasi-polyphonically (in the Isaac), can be handled in two possible ways: (1) with a similar timbre in all four parts or (2) with the melody in a contrasting color against the three lower parts.

Some comments on the various instruments themselves may be useful at this point in our discussion. Renaissance instruments of around 1500 are divided (according to medieval terminology) into two main groups: *haut* (high) and *bas* (low), referring not to pitch range but to higher and lower dynamic levels. Thus the *bas* group includes recorders, flutes, portative organ, krummhorns, viols, vielle, lute, and harpsichord. The *haut* group includes cornett, shawms, and sackbuts. All the *bas* instruments work well together, as do all the *haut* instruments. Cornett and sackbuts, normally *haut* instruments, are also welcomed into many *bas* scorings since they can be played relatively *piano* as well as *forte*.

Most of the instruments exist in complete "families" or consorts (soprano, alto, tenor, and bass). Scorings may use either the instruments of a particular family only (whole consort) or may include one or two instruments from several families (broken consort).

The members of the recorder family all play at "four foot" pitch—that is, an octave higher than written pitch. The complete consort is a very versatile ensemble, suitable for the instrumental performance of a vast quantity of Renaissance music. In vocal performance, the soprano recorder, which can be used to double soprano voices an octave higher, gives added brightness in lively pieces. This is also true when alto recorder doubles alto voices an octave higher. However, all such octave doublings add a certain thickness to the texture. Lower voice-parts should never be doubled an octave higher, but only in unison. (This is an exact parallel to orchestral scoring.) Alto voices can be doubled in unison by bass recorder, sopranos by tenor recorder. Unison recorder doubling gives a quiet, warm fullness to voices. (These comments apply also to the Renaissance flute and portative organ.)

Most recorders in use at present are modeled on Baroque instruments, although Renaissance recorders are now becoming available in this country. These latter instruments lack a full second octave; their compass is only an octave and a sixth. But because of the narrow ranges of the voice parts in most Renaissance music, this limit rarely presents any problem. Rather, the fuller sound of the Renaissance recorder (compared to the Baroque), and especially the fact that this fullness extends to the very bottom of its compass (unlike the tendency of the Baroque recorder to be weak in its lowest range), makes it far more suitable for the linearity of Renaissance music.

Since the recorder requires no embouchure technique, it is very easy to master in the beginning stages. Unfortunately this fact, and perhaps also a lack of awareness of the great potential of this instrument, has limited the development of some players. Although the recorder allows only small dynamic nuances, a good player (with a decent instrument) can achieve remarkable subtleties by the skillful combination of these slight dynamic shadings with different articulations. As with any wind instrument, a skillful and sensitive use of vibrato is an essential part of good playing. (See the comments under "Intonation.")

The krummhorn ("curved horn") has a double reed enclosed in a small air chamber. Since the player's lips or tongue never come in contact with the reed, it is not possible to achieve the second octave (the range is only a ninth). For the same reason there is no variation possible in the sound—only a very distinct beginning and end to each note. This inflexibility, combined with the krummhorn's buzzy sound, would be disastrous in the wrong piece. But it can be wonderful in the right place—for example, in a jaunty piece with distinctive rhythmic figures and repeated notes (see nos. 22, 24, 27, 28, 30, 32, and 39).

Of all the groups of Renaissance instruments, the bowed strings alone have some characteristics approaching those of the human voice. Though the total dynamic range is quite limited, the dynamic nuances and subtleties of articulation possible on viols make them suitable for many expressive pieces in which the less flexible recorder would be inadequate. Throughout the Renaissance, especially in sixteenth-century Italy and Elizabethan England, viols (and lute) were the favorite instruments for chamber-music making. With good players, a viol consort can be an elegant ensemble (see nos. 23a, 23b, 24, 26, 28, 29, 31, and 32). Viols also blend well when doubling with voices in a small vocal ensemble; they give the voices a slight edge and, in higher registers, an added focus (see nos. 2, 5, 16, 24, 35, and 39). They are especially effective for playing one or more instrumental parts accompanying a solo voice (see nos. 6, 8, 19, 20, 21, 22, 23a, 23b, 25, and 26).

The cornett, or cornetto, though it has the cup mouthpiece typical of brass instruments, is made of wood covered with leather. Its clean, exciting sound has no counterpart among modern instruments. Surviving contemporary accounts of performances glow with praise for this instrument as well as for its virtuoso players. During the sixteenth century, its slender cone shape was made either straight or slightly curved and in two sizes, one beginning at A below middle C, the other at E above middle C. It is the only wind instrument that never achieved a complete family, though a tenor cornett did appear during the sixteenth century. The cornett has a wide dynamic range. It can be played surprisingly softly (especially in its lower register) and can also produce a full *forte* (especially in its upper register). The cornett's ability to play softly makes it very useful in many *bas*-instrument scorings (see nos. 29 and 30). Although it is the most difficult to play of all the Renaissance wind instruments, a gifted player, willing to work diligently, can achieve outstanding results. Long the favored instrument for doubling the highest voices in performances of church music, it blends especially well with treble voices (see nos. 4, 5, 12, 27, and 37). It survived into the Baroque, and Bach calls for it to double the soprano line of the chorale in eleven cantatas.

The sackbut (from the fifteenth-century French *sacoueboute*, "pull-push"), direct ancestor of the trombone, was made in three sizes: alto, tenor, and bass. It has a narrower bore and a smaller bell than the trombone, which gives it a softer sound and greater agility. The slide allows the instrument equal command of all notes, unlike the shawms, which tend to have certain "problem" accidentals. The sackbut has a wide dynamic range, from a gentle, cantabile *piano* that blends perfectly with viols (see no. 29) to a resonant *forte,* and has outstanding control of dynamic nuance. For these reasons, sackbuts and cornetts are especially compatible (see nos. 28, 30, 32, and 41). Like the cornett, it blends well with voices; it was the usual instrument for doubling the lower voices in performances of sacred choral music, giving the voices a fullness and added clarity and providing a perfect foundation for the entire choral ensemble (see nos. 1, 3, 4, 5, 12, 13, and 17, as well as the secular pieces nos. 27 and 37; see also no. 35). Sackbuts work well in instrumental scorings with either cornetts or shawms (see nos. 28, 29, 30, 32, 38, and 41). These combinations are equally effective in pieces that are solemn, lively, or festive.

The shawm, the forerunner of the Baroque oboe, had grown to a complete family by the end of the fifteenth century and included all sizes from soprano (treble) to great bass. All have a compass of an octave and a sixth. The soprano and alto sizes are the most versatile members of the family. During the sixteenth century, the shawm was primarily an outdoor instrument, and every town had its shawm band to announce the arrival of a dignitary or the beginning of a tournament, to provide music for festivities, or to sound curfew. Depending a great deal on the reed being used as well as the expertise of the player, the shawm's basic *forte* dynamic level can be somewhat modified, permitting a range of dynamics from *forte* down to *mezzo piano*. The shawm's pungent, bright sound blends well with voices in choral performance, giving the vocal sound a bright edge and added focus (see nos. 1, 3, 4, 5, 12, 13, 17, 27, and 37). It also works well in various instrumental scorings with cornetts and sackbuts (see above). As with all double-reed instruments, attacks can be varied from gentle to pointed and instantaneous; thus the shawm is both suitable for legato playing, and especially effective for fast passages and lively, syncopated figures.

DYNAMICS, PHRASING, AND ARTICULATION

The fact that Renaissance instruments in general have considerably less dynamic range than either voices or modern instruments does not in any way mean that they have *no* dynamic possibilities. The dynamic limitations of the instruments must not be interpreted as permission to perform Renaissance music in a dynamic monotone. Many pieces do not need wide dynamic changes. What they do need is that the relatively small necessary changes, all perfectly possible, occur in the right places. Many of these smaller dynamic variations are a vital part of phrasing, which will be discussed below. A musical player on the recorder soon learns to use the limited dynamic resources of his instrument skillfully and effectively so that it sounds anything but wooden. Singers, who are not restricted by the limited dynamic range of the instruments, should never feel compelled to match the instruments in this respect. Certainly no singer ever felt it necessary to copy the absolutely unchanging dynamic level of the organ continuo in a Baroque aria. The entire problem of the skillful use of subtleties is carried to its limit by the organ and harpsichord, for neither of these instruments can make any note-to-note dynamic differences whatsoever. For organists and harpsichordists, finely controlled degrees of articulation and rhythmic freedom serve as quasi-abstractions of dynamic nuance. Yet these limited means, used skillfully and in the right places (for the music, after all, was conceived for this mode of performance), will create the illusion of dynamic nuance and will make the great solo literature composed for these instruments come alive.

It is essential, therefore, that both singers and instrumentalists become aware of the great expressivity possible in smaller and more limited dynamic differences and learn to use these effectively. If not, the great danger is that the intensely colorful sound we are used to in nineteenth-century music will trick us into giving performances in which, simply by contrast, the subtler dynamic nuances have eluded us, so that we are left with no dynamic shape at all and, therefore, no phrasing.

Although, as mentioned, many Renaissance pieces do not need—or want—a wide dynamic range, many choral pieces will certainly require a compass from *piano* to *forte*. This is especially true of long imitative movements with a wide variety of motives (see nos. 3 and 13). On the other hand, the predominantly lyric quality of other pieces will put the upper dynamic limit at *mezzo forte* (see nos. 5, 7, 8, 9, 10, 11, 15, and 35). Still other pieces will use an even narrower range: the gentle simplicity of Tromboncino's *Ave Maria* (no. 16) and Isaac's *Innsbruck* (no. 23) need hardly more than *piano* to *mezzo piano;* but Isaac's *Donna di dentro* (no. 37) must have a prevailing *forte,* relieved once or twice by a brief *mezzo forte*. Pieces that have several contrasting sections require yet another approach. Josquin's *Sanctus* (no. 4), for example, is typical of many Flemish Mass movements in that each individual section needs only a relatively narrow dynamic range; but the movement as a whole will certainly range from *piano* to *forte*. The markings in the individual sections of this movement might be *mp–mf, mp–mf, mf–f, p–mp*.

To a certain extent, dynamic contrasts are automatically built into choral music by the many shifts in the general vocal ranges throughout the piece as well as by the presence or absence of various voice parts at different points. Still, in addition to these "structural" dynamics, other dynamic changes should result from differences in the handling of the individual ideas in the music.

In performing Renaissance vocal music, we naturally look to the meanings of the text for clues about the general characteristics of the performance. But it is the text's word rhythms and phrase structures, and the way that these are fitted to the notes, that will tell us a great deal about the phrasing of the music. And what we learn confirms what our general musical instinct may already have told us, even though we were perhaps cautious in applying the information.

In gentle, flowing, and expressive pieces, we find almost invariably that the most important word (or the stressed syllable of the most important word) coincides with the strongest part (the goal or climax) of the phrase, usually the highest note. There may be one or two less important goal points along the way to and from the climax point. A typical expressive Renaissance phrase, then, follows a general ascent and descent. The dynamics, conforming to this, should gently increase and decrease, and the final note should be slightly softer than the notes just before it. In addition to this general dynamic shaping, a kind of added vocal "bloom" (a subtle crescendo or increase of warmth in the vocal sound) is needed during the climax note as well as during other notes that may occur at important points along the way to or from the climax note. These expressive "bloom" notes are often of longer value than the surrounding notes of the phrase.

Though the meter is always present as the underlying organization of pulses into regular groupings, the stronger and weaker points in the phrase occur independently of this underlying meter. A weak note may fall on the first beat of the measure, and a stronger one on the second or third beat; or a quarter note may fall on the beginning of a beat, followed by a half note that holds over into the next beat. Many cases of the latter must be treated as expressive offbeats, with the quarter note neutral but the half note more important and expressive. This "freedom from the bar line" is the essence of Renaissance phrasing (just as it is the essence of so much of the phrasing in Bach). The phrase, then, becomes a living, sensitive, pliant little event, with a beginning, important occurrences along the way, and a return to rest. The quick notes, which often occur here and there in expressive phrases, must neither be passed over too weakly nor given an awkward emphasis; they need a supple gracefulness.

In more vigorous, forthright pieces in moderate tempo as well as in all fast pieces the general shaping of phrases just described becomes more secondary, and the fundamental rhythmic vitality and inner drive of the music gain importance. These rhythmic factors will demand various degrees of accent on the important notes of the phrase (often not the highest note in fast pieces), and the separation of quarter and eighth notes. The word *separation,* however, must be qualified. On instruments, articulation will occur automatically. Good players will soon learn to control the degree of separation between the quicker notes. This should depend on the particular phrase, the tempo, and even the scoring. For singers, the matter is more complicated. When several quick notes are sung on one syllable, each note must receive a tiny, fresh pulse of sound, but usually without an actual interruption of sound between notes. When there is a new syllable for each note, the word sounds themselves provide an ideal means of articulation. Frequently a dotted quarter note is followed by a single eighth note. This presents no problem with instruments, but singers have a general tendency to absorb the single eighth note into the sound of the preceeding note, so that the eighth note is not properly heard. This problem will be avoided if the eighth note is given a fresh pulse of sound. In a large vocal group singing *forte* and fairly fast, these cases may require an actual short interruption of the sound just before the eighth note. The accented offbeats found in so many lively Renaissance pieces again illustrate the significance of the "freedom from the bar line". An all-important point to summarize about fast pieces—long notes and short notes should be treated in different ways: whole notes and half notes should have full length; quarters and eighths should be pulsed or detached and also slightly softer than the longer notes.

MUSICA FICTA

The unwritten tradition of *musica ficta* extended well back into the Middle Ages and persisted until around 1600. Although vocal compositions of the early Renaissance had few, if any,

accidentals indicated in the manuscripts, the performer was expected to add them in accordance with the traditions of *musica ficta*. During the course of the sixteenth century, stipulated accidentals appeared with increasing frequency, and the need for *musica ficta* ultimately disappeared.

Our first thought is to turn for information to the surviving writings of Renaissance theorists. Though some earlier writers do remark on it, theorists writing roughly between 1450 and 1525 (the period of most of the music in this book) discuss *musica ficta* very little; and the information we do have is in many ways unclear to us. Comparisons of the numerous lute arrangements of vocal pieces with their original versions have been instructive because lute tablature, unlike staff notation, shows the precise location on the fingerboard for all notes, and hence indicates accidentals (see no. 33 and Plate 6). Yet, for various reasons, this seemingly definitive source of information provides only clues and not final answers. The incompleteness of both of these avenues of information is further compounded by the surviving evidence that there were varying treatments of *musica ficta* in different regions and in different periods of time. It is small wonder, then, that this whole question remains a most controversial one among present-day scholars and performers.

But this uncertainty is still further and greatly compounded by yet another factor—a musical one. Any musician who has given serious thought to Renaissance music has discovered that while some accidentals having to do with leading tones, tritones, and cross relations seem unquestionably to be needed (though even here there are certain borderline cases), others are of a more or less optional nature. In fact, we are already told this by some of the earlier theorists, who divided *musica ficta* into two catagories: *causa necessitatis* (necessary) and *causa pulchritudinis* (not necessary, but desirable for the sake of beauty). Does not all of this, then, bring us back to the fundamental fact that Renaissance music, like any music, has traits in its personality that demand freedom and that will refuse to follow certain patterns in an always rigid, uniform way?

Although the musical language of the early Renaissance is modal, modifications of this language were already present in the fifteenth century that led to the emergence, and eventual supremacy, of the major-minor system. It is this interaction of the dawning major-minor system and the older modal tradition—an interaction sometimes subtle, sometimes obvious, sometimes unexpectedly complex, and sometimes purposefully ambiguous—that is central to the entire *musica ficta* question.

A few early twentieth-century scholars added accidentals in such wholesale fashion as to convert this rich subtlety of Renaissance music into a relatively bland version of major and minor. At the other extreme, some editors have suggested only the most absolutely essential accidentals—and sometimes not even all of these. The approach of the majority of scholars and performers today lies somewhere between these two extremes. The following is a very brief summary of the principal ways in which *musica ficta* has been applied in this book. Many accidentals must stand as essential; but many others—though certainly the preference of the editors of this collection—can be offered only as suggestions, for no amount of theoretical discussion can prove them either essential or inadmissable. (As is standard practice, all editorial accidentals are shown in small print over the note to which each applies.)

(1) In all cases of V–I or VII₆–I cadences, the appropriate note is raised to function as a leading tone. The "double-leading-tone" cadences found in certain Burgundian pieces have also been similarly created [2] (see no. 1, mm. 11, 19, 23; no. 35, mm. 4, 11, 18, and other places). However, for certain sylistic reasons not possible to discuss in this short space, the cadences in the anonymous English carol *Ave rex angelorum* (no. 7), a piece that has certain Burgundian features, have not been treated as double-leading-tone cadences.

(2) Tritones, both successive and simultaneous, as well as cross relations, have in many, but by no means all, cases been avoided by the use of accidentals.

(3) Most of the accidentals given in this book fall into one of the two categories just stated. Among the remaining ones, none of which can be considered essential, are the lowering of the sixth degree in important IV–V–I cadences in Dorian (as an analogy to the necessary flatting of the sixth degree to avoid the tritone in VI–V–I cadences in

this mode) and the raising of the minor third to major when it occurs as the final note of a piece or at the close of a large section.

Among the most interesting *musica ficta* problems are those that arise in pieces with a "mixed" or "partial" signature, fairly common in the early Renaissance. For a discussion of this question, as illustrated by Dufay's *Supremum est mortalibus* (no. 35), the reader is referred to the commentary on that piece (see also nos. 8 and 31).

ORNAMENTATION

As we have seen, the almost skeletal written version of a Renaissance piece is a far cry from what the listener of that time must have heard. We know that Renaissance performers frequently and freely added improvised ornamentation to the simpler, written version of the music. In fact, there is considerable evidence as far back as the twelfth century that even Gregorian chant was ornamented, and many of the more melismatic chants may perhaps be written-down ornamented versions of still earlier, simpler melodies. *Diminutio*, the sixteenth-century practice of dividing longer written notes into a profusion of shorter ones, fertilized not only the newly developing technique of variation, but the later keyboard toccata as well. The art of embellishment reached its climax in the large repertoire of systematized ornaments of late Baroque clavecin music and in the completely written-out melodic elaborations in many of Bach's slow movements. Ornamentation, written out but certainly in the spirit of improvisation, continued into the nineteenth century, especially in the more rhapsodic piano music of Chopin and Liszt.

Although ornamentation is mentioned by some medieval and early Renaissance theorists, it is not until the mid-sixteenth century that we get the first of a long line of detailed treatises on the subject, complete with many written-out examples showing simple melodic passages and various ways of ornamenting them. Although even the earliest of these treatises (Sylvestro Ganassi, *Opera intitulata Fontegara*, 1535; Diego Ortiz, *Tratado de glosas*, 1553) were published considerably later than the period spanned by this anthology, we may nevertheless take them as reasonably certain guides; modern scholars agree that theorists sum up musical practices already long in use. Even before these

---

[2] These cadences involve the simultaneous sharping of the fourth degree in the middle voice, thus avoiding a tritone between this voice and the leading tone in the top voice and, more important, resulting in a simultaneous leading tone to the fifth.

treatises began to appear, there were numerous arrangements for lute or keyboard of vocal pieces (see no. 34); and a comparison of these with their original vocal models can tell us a great deal about Renaissance ornamentation. We can briefly summarize the most general points on which the contemporary writers seemed to agree: (1) to use ornamentation sparingly (some writers deplored the excesses of performers); (2) to perform it flexibly, not mechanically; (3) to use it primarily on longer notes or the most important syllable; (4) to avoid it at the very beginning of a piece and to save the best for last; and (5) not to ornament two voice parts simultaneously. There was also a tradition of ornamenting sacred choral music, for which the virtuoso choirs of St. Mark's in Venice and St. Peter's in Rome were famous. But this highly specialized choral technique has not as yet been attempted even by the best present-day performing groups.

It is clear that no two performers ornamented the same piece in the same way—one glance at Ganassi's pages of examples proves this. And we can safely assume that the same performer ornamented the same piece differently from one performance to the next. But we are still faced with many puzzling questions: Were *all* Renaissance pieces ornamented? How *much* were they ornamented? Would there not be subtle differences of ornamentation resulting from the various idioms of keyboard, lute, bowed string, wind, and voice? Regarding this last point, it is interesting that Renaissance theorists made no distinction between vocal and instrumental ornamentation. And finally, could it be possible that the treatises, brimming with examples, give us a rather exaggerated idea of the importance of the whole question? Were there perhaps some fine performers who did *not* ornament?

Dufay's *Hostis Herodes* (no. 6) is itself a highly imaginative ornamentation of the simple chant melody and would seem (like Bach's written-out ornamentation) to be already complete, needing nothing more. But we find a similar melodic style in many other Burgundian pieces not based on pre-existing melodies. Perhaps the richly detailed melodic style in all of these pieces may be considered as already complete, written-out embellishment. If so, our analogy with Bach can go one step further, for Bach uses essentially the same highly embellished melodic style in some of his solo organ settings of chorale melodies as in

other movements where there is no pre-existing melody to be elaborated.

Are we then to wonder if perhaps only the plainest Renaissance music should be ornamented? The plainest (and simplest) piece in this anthology is Encina's *Triste España sin ventura* (no. 26). Certainly a sparing use of ornamentation on the top line would be suitable and effective for solo voice and would perhaps be essential in an instrumental performance, since no Renaissance instrument has the voice's ability to color sufficiently such a simple melodic line. Yet perhaps it is the utter simplicity of this piece that accounts for its restrained, poignant quality. If so, then more elaborate ornamentation would at least partly negate this quality. Other slow pieces in which ornamentation can give a heightened intensity and expressiveness are nos. 20, 25, and 29. Fast pieces in which ornamental figures in eighth and sixteenth notes can give an added delineation, zest, and excitement are nos. 28, 30, 32, and especially 38.

The conclusion to be drawn from the various evidence is that ornamentation must never sound as if it has been "pinned on" to the music, but rather must grow out of the line, be part of it. Many performers will find this very difficult to achieve readily. We have all grown up in the tradition of "later" music, already complete on the printed page, with no notes ever to be altered, added, or omitted and bearing varying quantities of the composer's own performance instructions, which we have been trained to carry out as best we understand them. But patience and experience will help, and, at least in the beginning, it may be necessary to write out the ornamentation. Though it cannot then qualify as being spontaneous, it will be in the very good company of the hundreds of pieces from all periods that are, in essence, written-down improvisation and from which we have all learned a great deal.

The various points discussed above make it obvious why no attempt was made in this anthology to offer any suggested ornamentation. To obtain concrete guidance, performers are uged to examine the various Renaissance treatises, to compare lute and keyboard arrangements of vocal pieces with the original models, and to consult some of the present-day writings on Renaissance ornamentation. A suggested list of readings is included at the end of this book.

PITCH AND TRANSPOSITION

The eight Gregorian modes, each with its one-octave range, together span a written pitch of nearly two octaves. But the notation of Gregorian chant was meant to show only the relative pitch of the notes in each mode, and had nothing to do with the actual sounding pitch. Thus all performances of chant, regardless of mode, would be pitched in approximately the same middle range comfortable for all the singers. By the end of the Reniassance, however, notation had developed to the point where notated pitch meant actual sounding pitch.

Early Renaissance notation represents a situation in between these two points. At this time, the Gregorian modes still served as the basic scale structures of the music; the later concept of "key" —that is, of a written transposition—existed in only a very limited way. For a piece in Dorian mode, for example, with its tonic on D, the only other possible written pitch was a fourth higher, using a signature of one flat. The other modes could be similarly transposed. Undoubtedly composers intended these transpositions to indicate at least an approximate higher or lower pitch level, for obviously the whole sonority of a piece is greatly affected by such a basic factor. These transpositions also tell us something about the general voice ranges intended by the composer (compare nos. 2 and 14 with no. 8). Yet it seems extremely likely, especially in many *a capella* performances, that the sounding pitch would have been somewhat different from either of the two possible written pitches, depending on the vocal ranges of the singers at hand.

Further complicating this whole question is the fact that there was no standardized actual sounding pitch during the Renaissance. The history of the various pitches in use at different periods of time, for different classes of instruments, and in different places is a very complicated subject, and one that is still not fully worked out. Even as late as the eighteenth century there were several pitches in use; individually, however, each one had by that time become more or less standardized. For the most part, performers today are spared the anxiety of these complexities, since almost all modern copies of Renaissance instruments are built to play at the present internationally standard $a' = 440$.

Thus we see that the written pitch in early Renaissance music is not sacred. Many Flemish pieces, especially those written in A.T.T.B. range, must be transposed upward if they are to be sung by an S.A.T.B. ensemble. The all-important thing is that the performing pitch should represent the *spirit* of the written pitch. Works like Ockeghem's Gloria (no. 2) and Josquin's *Absalon fili mi* (no. 14) were deliberately written in very low range; these pieces would have to be transposed higher for almost all vocal groups. But the transposition should be only enough to bring the voice parts within workable reach of the singers' vocal ranges yet still lie low in their ranges. In this way, the dark vocal color implied by the low pitch of the original notation will still be maintained.

VOCAL QUALITY

As mentioned earlier, the many Renaissance art works showing scenes of music making have given us a certain amount of valuable information about the performance of early music. But, like other avenues of information, this evidence is not complete or conclusive.

A good number of paintings of singers and instrumentalists together show that, while the instrumentalists' facial expressions look perfectly normal, the singers' faces have the kind of strained look that *could* indicate a tight, nasal vocal production. We cannot dismiss these renderings merely as artists' license, considering the scrupulous care taken by the painters to show details of all kinds realistically. Although we are probably not yet ready to hear Renaissance music sung with a nasal or otherwise strained vocal quality, we must still come up with a possible explanation of artistic depictions of Renaissance performances.

We should keep in mind that women's voices were never permitted in the sacred service, though they certainly sang secular music. The typical, highly trained chapel choir of around 1500 would have had approximately ten boy sopranos, and five each of countertenors, tenors, and baritones or basses. Well-trained boys' voices have a unique cleanness and solidity. Among the advantages of countertenors is that their voices are strong all the way to the bottom of the alto range.

None of this should be taken to imply that a mixed-voice ensemble is only second best, however, but rather as a guide to the kind of vocal sound that will work best for this music. Lighter-weight, trained voices are ideal, provided the vibrato is not obtrusive. But thirty-five or forty *untrained* voices, if carefully rehearsed and directed, can make a very good sounding chamber choir. A choir (or solo voice) that is good for Bach cantatas will do nicely for Renaissance vocal works. Just the same, large choruses, whose heavier and thicker sound is stylistically and historically wrong for Renaissance music, should not be deprived of this repertoire. If they perform it well, their members will be that much the richer, and no one in the audience will object.

INTONATION

Modern wind instruments play to a large extent automatically in tune, though certain notes may nevertheless need to be "humored." Renaissance instruments are far less perfected in this respect. They present sizable intonation problems, which good players will learn to solve. Many notes have to be adjusted in the playing. The player may also need to experiment with slight modifications on one or more finger holes of an instrument. Different types of reeds will have to be tried and discarded until a type is found that plays properly with the combination of the particular instrument and the individual player. On the recorder, unorthodox cross-fingerings may have to be found for certain notes. Viol players will find, in all likelihood, that some of their frets may need to be moved and retied, in order to bring all notes in tune.

All of these problems can—and must—be solved if performances of Renaissance music are to have any real worth. There is every reason to believe that Renaissance musicians had intonation standards just as rigorous as our own, and that these adjustments of instrumental pitch must have been a matter of course for performers of that time.

Mention should be made here of the various systems of meantone tuning that were used for keyboard instruments. Unlike equal temperament, this tuning is suitable only for the most commonly used simple keys. Its great advantage over equal temperament is that, within these keys, the common triads sound much purer. Because of the fact that the winds and the fretted strings play in an approximation of equal temperament, intonation adjustments will be necessary when these instruments play with meantone-tuned keyboard instruments.

MODERN INSTRUMENTS

In spite of the growing number of *collegia musica* at colleges and universities, there are still many madrigal groups, vocal ensembles, and chamber choirs that have no players of Renaissance instruments available to perform with them. While it is possible to perform almost all of the choral and part-song repertoire *a cappella,* much of it, as mentioned earlier, is far more effective with instrumental participation. If Renaissance instruments are not available, modern ones should be substituted.

Obviously, modern instruments are historically wrong for this music. But if the performers are fully aware of its general stylistic features, and especially if they have acquired (perhaps through recordings) a familiarity with the sounds and idiosyncracies of Renaissance instruments, the performance can certainly communicate the essential characteristics of the music. After all, there is probably even a greater difference between the modern piano and the eighteenth-century harpsichord than between the English horn and the shawm or the Boehm flute and the recorder; yet we have all heard some outstanding piano performances of Bach's harpsichord music. A skillful and gifted performer can translate this earlier language into terms suited to a modern instrument while recreating the essential characteristics of the older music.

All of the pieces in this collection for which we have suggested instrumental scorings also include a scoring for modern instruments. Flute substitutes for recorder, Renaissance flute, or portative organ; double reeds for Renaissance double reeds; trombone for sackbuts; violin, viola, and cello for viols; guitar for lute. Although the cup mouthpiece relates the modern trumpet to the cornetto, the heavier sound of the trumpet makes it unworkable in Renaissance scorings; flute is suggested instead as the most appropriate modern substitute. The krummhorn has no modern equivalent; however, the krummhorn or regal stop on a Baroque-style organ will give almost exactly the same sound.

A few words of caution are probably in order regarding the use of modern instruments. An understanding of Renaissance style and some familiarity with the sound of the early instruments will steer players (especially strings) away from some of the typical nineteenth-century playing traditions of modern instruments. Violinists and cellists should restrict themselves to more modest dynamic and color nuances and use only a gentle vibrato. But instrumentalists should never try literally to imitate the sound of viol, recorder, or harpsichord.

CONCLUSION

The foregoing discussion of the various questions and problems that confront the performer of Renaissance music has provided him with few answers, for, as we have seen, very few definite answers can be found. Indeed, this discussion may well have raised more questions than it has answered. As long as a musical tradition remains continuously viable and relevant, its users remain fluent in its (sometimes unwritten) language. As soon as that tradition dies, the language lapses and disappapears from memory. The symbols of a living tradition need be only suggestions; those of a vanished tradition can never be extensive enough. The surviving information about Renaissance performance is sketchy and incomplete; furthermore, no treatise, however explicit, can, alone, teach us "how to play."

Though the performance suggestions given with each piece in this collection naturally reflect the inevitable personal viewpoints and preferences of the editors, we have attempted to make our suggestions flexible enough for many differently constituted performing groups. In many cases alternate suggestions have been offered. All these should provide useful guidance also for the performance of pieces not included here. But the performer must remember that the recommendations given here are still only suggestions. This book alone cannot teach us "how to play" either. We must certainly examine carefully information we do have and apply it intelligently to each piece in turn. But in the final analysis, it is the music itself that must remain the best guide to a convincing performance.

A carefully, thoroughly educated musical instinct must be drawn upon to its fullest, because it is this general musical experience that will tell us that all music must be phrased and articulated; that every composition has its particular structural techniques that must determine many aspects of its performance; that every piece has a particular shape; that every performance is made with sounds, and that not only must these accurately convey the composer's intention, but they must also please the ear. Though Isaac's musical language is as different from Mozart's as is Mozart's from Wagner's, there can be no "double standard" in the performance of any of their music. The greatest creative musicians of all periods are on the same level, and the performance of all of their music deserves the very best we can give.

PART I ❧

THE ORDINARY OF THE MASS

The Mass, the central and most solemn act of worship in the Catholic liturgy, is the mystical re-enactment of the Lord's Supper. Its rich and varied text ranges from the divine mystery of Christ's birth through the despair of His death to the splendor of heavenly rejoicing. From the anonymous fourteenth-century *Messe de Tournai* and the extraordinary Mass of Guillaume de Machaut to the Mass of Igor Stravinsky, this text has been set to music more often than any other single text in the history of Western civilization.

The structure of the Mass, which evolved over several centuries and has remained in its present form since the early Middle Ages, includes both sung and recited sections. Some of the sung portions remain constant for every day of the church year. These unchanging parts, called the Ordinary, include the Kyrie (a plea for mercy), the Gloria (expressing glory to God the Father and asking mercy of God the Son), the Credo (a summary of the most central Christian beliefs), the Sanctus (an ancient prayer of praise and exaltation), and the Agnus Dei (a plea for the forgiveness of sins and for eternal peace). The remaining parts of the sung Mass—the Proper—are different for each day or feast of the church year.

Though many of the Proper texts were set by various composers, it was the Ordinary that was set most frequently.

A large number of Gregorian melodies for the Ordinary gradually came into use during the early centuries of the church. Many of these served Renaissance composers as structural scaffolds for entire Masses, providing clear cyclical relationships between the Mass movements. Other Renaissance Masses were built around folk songs. Still others used a chanson tenor or even a complete chanson or motet. Such borrowings showed the high esteem in which certain pieces were held, and some pieces became favorites for Masses.

A setting of the Mass Ordinary was the standard large musical form in the Renaissance, much as the symphony was in the Classic and Romantic periods. The imagination of the Renaissance musician was not fettered by the unchanging text of the Mass. To the great composer of any era, a strictly prescribed format is challenge and inspiration, not limitation, and some of the Renaissance Masses are among the creative masterpieces of all time.

1

GUILLAUME DUFAY (c. 1400–1474)

Kyrie (Mass fragment)

The highly mannered intricacies of the last decades of the *Ars nova* around 1400 held little interest for the new young generation of composers. The endless fascination with complex constructions and layered embellishments had run its course. In the music of Guillaume Dufay, the greatest composer of his time, a new synthesis emerged. Dufay used the structural techniques of the late Middle Ages with the warm lyricism of fourteenth-century Italy and the English euphony of John Dunstable to produce a new style, characterized by clear textures, simple but strong harmonic structures, and above all rich melodic grace. This fresh and graceful style, as developed by succeeding generations of composers, became the central musical language of Europe for more than a hundred years.

Born in Flanders around 1400, Dufay was among the first of many northern composers to work for a considerable part of his life in Italy. He spent several periods of time there, at the court of the Malatesta family at Rimini as well as at the papal chapel. His thorough acquaintance with Italian music of the late thirteenth and early fourteenth centuries certainly dates from these periods. His later life was spent in his native France as canon of Cambrai Cathedral, where he composed new music for the cathedral's repertory and supervised its performance. From the Burgundian court to that of the Medici in Florence his music had won him great fame. Consequently, more and more students came to study with the now internationally esteemed master, and Cambrai became one of the most brilliant centers of music in the north.

Dufay wrote music in every genre current in his day. In addition to eight complete extant Masses, eighty-odd motets, and over sixty secular pieces, there are thirty-five Mass fragments, among which is the short but powerful Kyrie presented here. The almost classic simplicity of this piece is typical of much of Dufay's earlier sacred music. The writing is *a 3* and the total pitch span is less than two octaves. The tenor and contratenor lie in the same range, with the contratenor sometimes crossing below the tenor to function as the lowest part. The bold, almost stark sonority of this piece, so characteristic of many three-voice compositions of the late Middle Ages and early Renaissance, results in part from the plain melodic style and the frequent omission of the third in the harmony. Although the voices move together in a compelling triple-meter rhythm and the piece has a very strong harmonic outline, the writing is in no sense chordal since the individual voice parts have the utmost freedom of melodic contour. It is these shapely melodic lines that help to obscure the fact that the piece is made up of nine consecutive four-measure phrases (the last of these extended by three measures), complete with a cadence on each fourth measure.[1] The nine

---

1 The simple, nine-phrase plan of this movement results from Dufay's literal treatment of the text, in which the invocations "Kyrie eleison," "Christe eleison," and "Kyrie eleison" occur three times each. Until about 1400, composers generally retained this ninefold form in settings of this text. But after about 1420, this inherently rigid format was largely abandoned in favor of the much more flexible approach of three larger, continuous sections. The earlier and later approaches may be outlined as: aa'a"bb'b"cc'c' versus ABC.

cadences in themselves (including those with double leading tones, as in mm. 11 and 19) serve as a fairly representative sampling of cadential formulas as used by Dufay and his contemporaries.

This Kyrie is most effectively performed when the top line is sung by countertenors, thus rendering all three parts in male vocal timbre (though of course, altos may be used instead). Because both the tenor and contratenor lie in the same high baritone range and must have equal weight, both parts should be sung by a mix of tenors and baritones. Performance is equally effective with or without instrumental doubling. (Suggested scorings are given below.) Some contrast is desirable for the middle section: if instruments are used, let them be *tacet* in the Christe; if the piece is performed *a cappella,* the Christe should be sung by solo voices. The performance must not inadvertently emphasize the four-measure phrase-structure sequence by giving any hint of a stop or rest on each of the "-son" syllables. Rather, the piece must be taken as three larger sections, with the three short phrases within each section only subtly articulated and the increased rhythmic excitement of the final phrase highlighted.

SOURCE: Bologna, Bibl. G. B. Martini, Cod. Q 15, fol. 151.
MODERN EDITION: *Dufay, *Opera omnia,* ed. H. Besseler, IV, Rome, 1962, p. 3.
PERFORMANCE SUGGESTIONS: ♩ = c. 108
  NUMBER OF VOICES: nine to eighteen.
    S. countertenors (or altos)   with alto shawm
    Ct. tenors and baritones   with tenor shawm or tenor sackbut
    T. tenors and baritones   with tenor shawm or tenor sackbut
  MODERN SCORING:
    S. with English horn
    Ct. with trombone or bassoon
    T. with trombone or bassoon

Kyrie (Mass fragment)

2 ❧

JOHANNES OCKEGHEM (c. 1420–c. 1495)

Gloria, from *Missa Sine nomine*

In the generation following Dufay, most composers were at their best in chansons, which survive in such large numbers in the beautifully decorated manuscript collections of the time. The notable exception is Ockeghem, the greatest master of the period, who, though the composer of some exquisite chansons, left us a good number of outstanding motets and Mass settings.

Born around 1420, he was a chorister at various times at the Church of Our Lady in Antwerp, the chapel of Duke Charles of Bourbon, and the French royal chapel. Frenchman first and last, he never went to Italy; his long working life was spent in the service of three French kings: Charles VII, Louis XI, and Charles VIII. The high regard in which he was held by his contemporaries and pupils is attested to by Josquin's beautiful and moving *Déploration* on his death.

Ockeghem, though certainly influenced by Dufay, created a highly individual style that could never be mistaken for that of any other composer. The clear, tonally directed phrase structures of Dufay are often conspicuously avoided by Ockeghem in favor of long, soaring, rhapsodic lines; and although these lines permeate the entire fabric of all the voice parts, there is usually very little imitation. Cadences (and their resulting harmonic profiling) tend to be minimized by the fact that phrases begin and end at totally independent times in the different voice parts. It is this overlapping, seamless texture that gives Ockeghem's music its uniquely flowing quality. Many of his works (including the Gloria given here) explore the dark sonorities of low ranges, and have a restless, brooding autumnal quality. (For a work by Ockeghem with a totally different sonority, see no. 9.)

Our Gloria, from the *Missa Sine nomine,* which is based on the Gloria from the Gregorian Mass XV, is in some respects very untypical of Ockeghem. The unusually plain melodic style of this piece may be due to the fact that it is a paraphrase, shared by all three upper voices, of an essentially syllabic chant.[1] (Cf. Ockeghem's paraphrase technique in no. 9.) The striking passages in chordal style (such as mm. 43–49), which seem to foreshadow those later composed with such mastery by Josquin, are also rarely found in Ockeghem's music.

We have no certain knowledge of how pitches actually sounded in Ockeghem's day. Musical notation in the early Renaissance was still largely a system of relative rather than fixed pitch notation. A piece in the Phrygian mode (like this Gloria) could be written at only one of two pitch levels: either as done here, with the final on E, or in transposed Phrygian a fourth higher, with a signature of B flat and the final on A. Therefore, some latitude regarding the actual sounding pitch seems inevitable in order to accommodate the singers' ranges. If the ensemble is blessed with exceptionally low basses, there is every reason to perform this piece at its written pitch. If very low basses are not available, it will be necessary to transpose the piece a whole tone or a minor third higher. This transposition, though still keeping the top line in countertenor

---

[1] *Liber Usualis,* Tournai, 1963, p. 57. The notes of the chant melody are indicated in the score by small crosses.

range, will bring it into better range for altos. Though some of the dark sonority will be lost, the improvement of the vocal ranges will more than compensate. A bright, well-focused vocal quality, especially in the lower parts, will help to avoid any excessive "thickness" in places where the *vagans* and bass move in thirds in very low register. Performance by mixed voices is also a valid alternative. In that case, if the piece is pitched a third or a fourth higher, it can be sung by sopranos, altos, tenors, baritones, and basses. (For a fuller discussion of performance pitch, see the Introduction, p. 12.)

SOURCE: Rome, Biblioteca Vaticana, Chigiana Cod. C. VIII, fol. 234.

MODERN EDITION: *Ockeghem, *Collected Works*, ed. D. Plamenac, Philadelphia, 1966, II, p. 77.

PERFORMANCE SUGGESTIONS: ♩ = c. 60

NUMBER OF VOICES: fifteen to twenty-five, with or without instrumental doubling.

I—*At written pitch or a tone higher:*

S.	countertenors (or altos)	with treble or tenor viol
Ct.	tenors	with tenor viol
T.	baritones	with tenor or bass viol
V.	basses	with bass viol
B.	basses	with bass viol

II—*A minor third or fourth higher:*

S.	sopranos	with treble viol
Ct.	altos	with treble or tenor viol
T.	tenors	with tenor viol
V.	baritones	with tenor or bass viol
B.	basses	with bass viol

NOTE: The organ can be used instead of viols. Suggested registration: *gedeckt* 8-ft. and 4-ft. for the three upper parts; a soft 8-ft. reed for the two lower parts.

MODERN SCORING: Modern string instruments can be substituted for viols, but see the Introduction, p. 14, regarding their use in Renaissance music.

Gloria, from *Missa Sine nomine*

Johannes Ockeghem

3

JACOB OBRECHT (c. 1450–1505)

Credo, from *Missa Fortuna desperata*

The generation born around 1450 included an extraordinary number of outstanding composers. Jacob Obrecht, the only real Dutchman among the leading masters of the period was perhaps the finest of them all after Josquin himself.[1] As a church musician, he was active at Utrecht, Bergen-op-Zoom, Cambrai, Bruges, and Antwerp. He went to Ferrara—that dazzling center for music under Hercules I—at the duke's invitation. (Josquin also spent part of his career in Hercules' employ.) He died of the plague in 1505.

Obrecht composed twenty-seven Masses, all cyclic, several based on chansons, and all employing *cantus firmus* technique in many ingenious ways. In addition to its clear harmonic and tonal organization, much of the time in what we would today call the major or minor modes, the most noticeable feature of Obrecht's music is its pervading use of imitation. In fact, credit for fully establishing the technique of imitative counterpoint—which was to become the foundation stone of sixteenth-century musical style—must be shared by Obrecht and Antoine Busnois. Other frequently found traits of Obrecht's music are: voices moving in parallel tenths, scalewise figures, sequences, and many short stretches of writing *a 2*. Obrecht is the first composer known by name to have written a considerable number of purely instrumental pieces.

In the *Missa Fortuna desperata*, Obrecht uses as his tenor *cantus firmus* the tenor part of Busnois's famous chanson (see no. 29), manipulating it in several ingenious ways. In the Credo,

he uses the second half of Busnois's tenor backward (in retrograde), then the first half of the tenor in normal sequence. At the "Et incarnatus," he repeats this plan, a repetition identical in every detail, including the same number of measures of rest in the *tacet* sections. Such a seemingly arbitrary, not to say downright whimsical, structural plan is not unlike the *cantus firmus* manipulations found in some of his other Masses. One might well think that a careful examination of this rigid, predetermined arrangement of the tenor part—especially in view of the second half of the movement where the entire scheme is repeated intact with its *tacets*—would surely provide clues to the musical development within the piece. But one very soon finds that the whole polyphonic matrix unfolds paying only casual attention to the tenor *Cantus firmus*. Many factors combine to give this impression: the various entrances of the *cantus firmus* do not coincide with (or cause) any new subsection beginnings (if, indeed, one can even find subsection beginnings in such a continuous polyphonic texture); in some places, the *cantus firmus* is moving in note values similar to those of the other parts; and, finally, half the time we are hearing the *cantus firmus* melody backward. This set of conditions goes a long way in drastically de-emphasizing the formerly independent life of Busnois's melody. Obrecht has worked things so that the pre-existing borrowed melody—the very lifespring of the piece—gives the impression of an innocent fourth part "along for the ride." The one element that does help to make the tenor part sound like a *cantus firmus* is its *tacets*.

[1] G. Reese, *Music in the Renaissance*, rev. ed., New York, 1959, p. 186.

These silences make us, in one way, more aware of it than if it were present all the time.

All of this may help in making basic decisions about the performance of this work. Should the *prius factus* tenor part be in some way set off from the other voice parts? (Certainly this is the case with the vast majority of *cantus-firmus-based* compositions.) In view of the factors just mentioned, it would seem very advisable *not* to emphasize the *cantus firmus,* but to handle it in essentially the same way as the other parts.

The many eighth-note figures in all parts, which contribute so much to the rhythmic excitement of the piece, must be absolutely clear and articulated. The suggested "Relaxed" at the "Et incarnatus" is meant to indicate only a slight slowing of the tempo, so that the driving, rhythmic quality of the piece can, in this section, give way to a more lyric quality. A more significant slowing of the tempo is not possible here (in spite of the liturgical meaning in this section of the Credo) because of the overriding factor of the movement's homogeneous structure.

At the written pitch, this piece works perfectly for countertenors (or altos), tenors, tenors, and basses. That the two inner parts lie in the same range and frequently cross is the norm in much of the music of this period. Performance a tone higher will be better for altos, and probably for basses also, but will be a little less ideal for tenors. Performance by S.A.T.B. is possible only if the piece is transposed up a fourth, giving ideal soprano range and good baritone/bass range. At this pitch it will be necessary to assign a mix of altos and tenors to the two inner parts, in order to accommodate the range of these parts and to give them equal weight. In addition, some of the singers may need to be routed between the two parts. All such switches should involve only some of the singers in each section, and should never be done for less than a complete melodic phrase unit.

SOURCE: *Missae Obrecht,* Petrucci, Venice, 1503.

MODERN EDITION: *Obrecht, Opera omnia,* ed. A. Smijers, Amsterdam, 1953, I, fasc. 3, pp. 132–142.

PERFORMANCE SUGGESTIONS: $\downarrow$ = c. 88

NUMBER OF VOICES: sixteen to thirty-two.

I—*At written pitch or a tone higher:*

S.	countertenors (or altos)	with alto shawm
A.	tenors	with tenor sackbut or tenor shawm
T.	tenors	with tenor sackbut or alto shawm
B.	basses	with bass sackbut

II—*Transposed a fourth higher:*

S.	sopranos	with treble shawm
A.	altos/tenors	with alto shawm or alto sackbut
T.	altos/tenors	with alto sackbut or alto shawm
B.	baritones/basses	with bass or tenor sackbut

NOTE: It is suggested that the instruments be *tacet* from m. 110 to mm. 141/142, and that this section be performed with solo voices or semichorus.

MODERN SCORING:

I—S. with English horn
A. with bassoon
T. with trombone or bassoon
B. with trombone

II—S. with oboe
A. with English horn
T. with English horn
B. with trombone or bassoon

Credo, from *Missa Fortuna desperata*

Jacob Obrecht

4 〰

JOSQUIN DES PREZ (c. 1445–1521)

Sanctus, from *Missa Gaudeamus*

"He is the master of the notes; they must do as he wills. As for the other composers, they have to do as the notes will." Though Martin Luther's admiring assessment of Josquin, his great Flemish contemporary, was echoed throughout sixteenth-century Europe, many details of the composer's life are still a mystery. It is generally agreed that he was born about 1445 in the province of Hainaut in northwest France and was apparently a choirboy at the Collegiate Church at St. Quentin.

Then the lure of Italy drew him, as it did so many of the northern musicians of his day. He became a member of the choir at Milan Cathedral, and in 1472 went to the chapel of Duke Galeazzo Maria Sforza. He remained in the service of the Sforza family for several years, even after the duke's murder in 1476. For at least eight years (1486–1494[?]) he was a member of the famous papal chapel, which provided musical employment to generations of Renaissance composers.

After spending some time in France, he was summoned back to Italy by Duke Hercules I of Ferrara. The duke had been advised to engage Isaac rather than Josquin as his *maistro della capelle*, because "Isaac is able to get on with his colleagues better and composes new pieces more quickly. It is true that Josquin composes better, but he does it when it suits him and not when one wishes him to. Furthermore, Josquin asks 200 ducats while Isaac is pleased with 120." Josquin was awarded the post, however, and he remained in Ferrara (where he composed the famous *Missa Hercules Dux Farrariae* in honor

of his patron) at least until the death of Hercules in 1505.

During the composer's last years, which saw the publication of most of his music, he may have been at the brilliant Flemish court of Margaret of Austria; later he was at the court of Louis XII in Paris. Productive to the end of his long life, he died in 1521 at Condé-sur-l'Escaut. To his own age he was *omnium princeps;* to succeeding ages he is the greatest of all the composers of the Renaissance.

Taken as a whole, Josquin's Masses, motets, and chansons show an extraordinary range of expression, from the most lighthearted playfulness (often with obscene texts so typical of the period) to the darkest mourning and penitence. One way or another, all of his Masses use the well-established contemporary techniques of handling pre-existent material. In the *Missa Gaudeamus,* based on the Gregorian Introit *Gaudeamus . . . Mariae,*[1] the entire borrowed melody appears in some movements as a *cantus firmus,* though more often only the opening six notes (set to the word "Gaudeamus") are used. Arranged in various mensural patterns and sometimes elaborated, these six notes serve as the motivic germ which permeates the entire work.

In the opening section of the Sanctus, the six-note motive appears as a short *cantus firmus* phrase in the highest voice. Stated three times, like a heavenly ostinato, it soars over the restless polyphony of the three lower parts. Typical of

---

1 *Liber Usualis,* Tournai, 1963, pp. 1556, 1675. For a polyphonic setting of the Introit itself, see no. 12.

the Masses of Josquin and of the early Renaissance in general, the "Pleni" and "Benedictus" sections are composed *a 2* or *a 3* and do not make use of the borrowed material. In the "Hosanna," the six-note motive, elaborated, is stated by each part in turn as it enters. But, except in the alto part, these are to be the only appearances of this motive; the other three parts develop a completely new motive, while the alto reiterates the "Gaudeamus" motto as an insistant ostinato.

The movement beautifully illustrates Josquin's typical musical response to the various ideas of his text. In this piece, with its very short but highly contrasted text, the "Sanctus" music is broad, warm, flowing; the "Pleni" is lighter and more agile; the "Hosanna," boisterous, energetic, jubilant; the "Benedictus," calm, thoughtful, tender. Though Josquin was certainly not the first composer to project textual meaning through the music, he was the first to do so almost consistently in every piece. In his best Masses—always cyclic, with all the movements germinating from a single melodic seed—Josquin discovered the means to bring forth from that single seed a whole range of musical expression—now pleading, now adoring, now rejoicing.

The vocal ranges lie well for sopranos, countertenors (or altos), tenors, and basses, but because the alto part lies very low for alto voices, a few tenors would be needed with them also. The tricky rhythmic interplay in the "Pleni" (typical of many of Josquin's two- and three-voice Mass sections) demands the greatest clarity. This, plus the reduction in sonority resulting from the dropping of one voice part, strongly suggests solo voices (or a very small group) for this section. Similarly, the gentle, two-voice "Benedictus" is especially suitable for solo voices; and, if performed this way, it stands out all the more effectively between the two full "Hosanna" statements. This work can certainly be performed *a capella*, but it is probably most effective with winds doubling the voices in the *tutti* sections. This scoring also enhances the *tutti-solo-tutti-solo-tutti* symmetry of the piece.

This movement illustrates the principle of proportional tempo relationships, found in so many works by Josquin and his contemporaries. Each of the various mensural signs used in the earlier Renaissance indicated not only meter (like a modern time signature), but also—where several different mensural signs occur in the course of the same piece—the relative *tempo* of the different sections as well. In this Sanctus, the "Hosanna" should go twice as fast as the "Pleni," and, in the "Benedictus," one measure is to equal one measure of the "Hosanna." We suggest that the opening "Sanctus" be taken at ♩ = 60, with the slightly faster ♩ = 64 for the "Pleni." In this case, the "Hosanna" will go at ♩ = 128, which in turn will give ♩ = 86 for the "Benedictus." This provides a perfect tempo for the "Hosanna," but the "Benedictus" will sound rushed. If the "Benedictus" is taken a little slower (♩ = 80), the general proportion will still be observed, and the spirit of the music can come through. It must be added that many of the original mathematical proportions are impossible in actual performance, and therefore adjustments will frequently be necessary for musical reasons (see no. 35). See the Introduction, pages 2–3, for further comments on this whole subject.

SOURCE: *Missae Josquin,* Petrucci, Venice, 1502.

MODERN EDITION: *Josquin des Prez, *Werken,* ed. A. Smijers, *Missen,* I, Amsterdam, 1926, pp. 72 ff.

PERFORMANCE SUGGESTIONS: ♩ = c. 60; ♩ = c. 64; ♩ = c. 128; ♩ = c. 80

NUMBER OF VOICES: sixteen to thirty-two, preferably with instrumental doubling in the "Sanctus" and "Hosanna" sections.

S. sopranos	with cornetto
A. countertenors, or altos plus a few tenors	with alto shawm
T. tenors	with tenor sackbut or alto shawm
B. basses	with bass sackbut

MODERN SCORING:
S. with flute
A. with English horn
T. with English horn or bassoon
B. with trombone or bassoon

Sanctus, from *Missa Gaudeamus*

Josquin des Prez

Repeat Hosanna

5

HEINRICH ISAAC (c. 1450–1517)

Agnus Dei, from *Missa De Martyribus*

Heinrich Isaac, who divided his life between Italy, Germany, and Austria, and whose career took him to the leading courts of Europe, stands as the very archetype of the widely traveled, and royally supported Renaissance composer. He was born about 1450 in Brabant or East Flanders, but no information has survived about the first part of his life.

He first arrived in Florence—for the rest of his life his favorite city—in about 1484, and began his service as a composer to the brilliant Medici court of Lorenzo the Magnificent. He was also music teacher to Lorenzo's children—among them the future Pope Leo X—as well as organist at the churches of Sta. Maria del Fiore and the Annunziata. In the aftermath of the overthrow of the Medici by the fierce zealot Savonarola, Isaac left Florence, and in 1497 he became court composer to the Emperor Maximilian I in Vienna. In Maximilian, he found a patron equal to Lorenzo, and one who permitted him frequent leaves to travel. He spent much time at the emperor's country estate at Innsbruck as well as at Constance and Ferrara. He finally returned to his beloved Florence, still receiving a stipend from Maximilian, and died there in 1517.

The *Choralis Constantinus* (see no. 12) is Isaac's monumental collection of settings of the Proper for all Sundays of the church year as well as certain feasts. The entire cycle concludes with five settings of the Ordinary of the Mass; one of these is the *Missa De Martyribus*. All five are *alternatim* Masses—that is, only portions of the text have been set polyphonically, leaving the remaining sections to be sung in chant. The polyphonic sections are always based on those portions of the chant that they replace. It is this thematic connection between chant and polyphony that gives an *alternatim* movement its particular kind of structural unity. The *alternatim* idea, long established by Isaac's time, has, at its core, the simple but aesthetically satisfying principle that monophony and polyphony, coexisting in the same piece, mutually enhance each other.

This exquisite miniature, framed by its two chant statements, should be performed in a warm, flowing manner, with a gentle shaping of the rises and falls of the melodic lines. The soprano and tenor voices, which paraphrase the chant melody, are in canon throughout, but it is best not to emphasize this at the expense of the sensitive and perfectly balanced four-part writing. Nevertheless, subtle emphasis of the canon is desirable. As in so many canonic pieces, both Renaissance and Baroque, the composer's art is such that the canonic voice is seemingly slipped in when one is not looking—as though the canon were almost an accident. (Perhaps the ultimate example of this is the series of canons in Bach's *Goldberg Variations*.)

SOURCE: *Choralis Constantinus*, III, Formschneider, Nuremberg, 1555.
MODERN EDITION: *Isaac, *Five Polyphonic Masses*, ed. L. Cuyler, Ann Arbor, Mich., 1956, pp. 116 f.
PERFORMANCE SUGGESTIONS: ♩ = c. 58

NUMBER OF VOICES: twelve to sixteen.

S.	sopranos	with tenor recorder (or treble viol)
A.	countertenors or altos	with tenor or treble viol (or bass recorder)
T.	tenors	with tenor or bass viol
B.	basses	with bass viol

For from sixteen to thirty-two voices. the following scoring is suggested:

S.	with cornetto (or treble shawm)
A.	with alto shawm
T.	with tenor sackbut (or tenor shawm)
B.	with bass (or tenor) sackbut

MODERN SCORING:

S.	with flute
A.	with English horn
T.	with bassoon or English horn
B.	with bassoon

Agnus Dei, from *Missa De Martyribus*

[1] From the *Graduale Pataviensi,* Basel, 1511. A photostat was kindly provided by Professor Edward R. Lerner and transcribed by Professor Joseph Ponte, both of Queens College of the City University of New York. The chant melody is shown a fourth higher than the original to agree with Isaac's transposition of the mode. Isaac's setting is based on the second of the three Agnus Dei chant statements. This statement begins as follows

but from "qui tollis" on is identical to the first and third statements. Crosses are used to mark the notes of the chant in the polyphony.

PART II ∾

SHORTER LITURGICAL AND DEVOTIONAL PIECES

In addition to the unchanging Ordinary of the Mass, a vast number of liturgical and nonliturgical sacred texts, spanning the entire church year and embracing the whole gamut of human emotion, led Renaissance composers to produce a great variety of shorter sacred pieces. Many Mass Propers were set, to be performed during Mass on the appropriate day; at other times, a composer might set only one portion of a Proper, leaving the remaining parts to be sung in chant. The four Marian antiphons, sung during Compline, were favorite liturgical texts, as was the Magnificat. The Psalms, or portions of them, provided a rich treasury of texts for motets that could be sung as additional adornments to the Mass. The Gregorian hymns offered abundant source material for new compositions based on these melodies.

What a musical feast Mass must have been at Maximilian's chapel, with Isaac directing one of the newly published Masses of Josquin, his own Proper for the feast of the day, an interpolated hymn or motet by the rather old-fashioned but highly regarded Dufay, and a few "incidental" pieces played on cornetts and sackbuts.

In contrast to this royal splendor, the many private chapels made use of nonliturgical pieces for private devotional services. These pieces, often in a simple, songlike style, needed only a modest number of performers and were intended for popular use as well. In Italy, vernacular devotional songs called *laude* were composed in the style of the newly popular secular songs. In England, the attractive and folklike carols were used for festive and processional occasions. And in Germany, the ancient folk hymns called *leisen* served liturgical as well as popular functions.

6 ✧

GUILLAUME DUFAY (c. 1400–1474)

Hostis Herodes

The cycle of hymn settings that Dufay wrote for the papal choir around 1430 was widely known and very popular during the composer's lifetime. In fact, the hymns were still in use seventy years later; witness the appearance of most of them in the manuscript Cappella Sistina 15, dating from around 1500.

All of Dufay's hymns are intended for *alternatim* performance, the even-numbered verses to be sung in his polyphonic settings and the odd-numbered ones to the original chant melody. For these polyphonic verses, Dufay chose the paraphrase technique that his English and Burgundian forbears had found so attractive—that is, to ornament the chant melody and place it in the top part. The result of this technique is to transform the ancient chant tunes into melodic lines in the composer's own style. In their warm, shapely cantilena, the chant-derived top parts of these hymns are very little different from the treble parts of his own original chansons.

The lovely Phrygian melody *Hostis Herodes* is the Vespers hymn for Epiphany (January 6); the same tune, with a different text (*A solis ortus cardine*), serves as the Lauds hymn at Christmas. Dufay's setting is very faithful to the chant framework. His few extended ornamental melismas are chiefly reserved for the correspondingly expressive places in the chant (as on "*im*-pi-e", and "mor-ta-li-*a*"). On the final vowel of "mortalia," there is a glowing *fauxbourdon* passage (mm. 18–20), set as a melisma in all three voices.

Dufay's compositions *a 3* (including *Hostis Herodes*) are basically two-voice structures consisting of the highest voice (*superius*) and tenor.

Because the elaborated *superius* is melodically the richer part, the well-known label "treble-dominated style" is a very accurate one. The third voice, the contratenor, moving in the same range as the tenor (and both lying an octave below the *superius*), serves to fill out the texture and complete the harmony. However, whenever the tenor ascends to the upper part of its range, the contratenor drops below it, serving now as the lowest part and creating root-position harmonic progressions that do not exist in the two-voice framework (see mm. 2–4, 7–13, 15–17, 22–23). Because of this somewhat utilitarian nature, the contratenor is less graceful than the other parts.

In most of Dufay's hymns, we find text underlay given only for the chant-elaborated part, with *incipits* for the other parts. Unfortunately, the sometimes perplexing question of whether to perform a particular part vocally or instrumentally is by no means always settled by the presence or absence of text (see the Introduction, pp. 3–4). It is perfectly conceivable that one could add text to the lower parts of these hymns, as is the case with several that appear in the Sistine manuscript mentioned above, and to perform all three parts vocally. (Gerber's excellent edition, on which ours is based, presents the hymns with all parts texted.) But it is our belief that a more convincing performance results when only the chant elaboration is sung, with the other two parts performed instrumentally.

The chant verses should be sung by from four to sixteen men's voices, with the polyphonic verses sung by solo voice. Countertenor is ideal, either at written pitch or a tone lower; alto or mezzo-soprano soloist would also be suitable. For soprano voice, the pitch must be raised a minor third, with the chant sung by tenors. Because of the gentle character of this piece, the only suitable instruments for the lower parts are either tenor and bass viols, or organ. On a Baroque-style organ, 8' only might be sufficient; but on the more standard American organ, 8' with soft 4' or even soft 2' will be advisable. In any case, the two parts should have contrasting registrations. Above all, this lovely piece should be performed with warmth and shaping in the vocal part and a suppleness in the instrumental parts, particularly with regard to the many gentle offbeats.

SOURCE: Bologna, Civico Museo Bibliografica Musicale, Cod. 37, fol. 288. [See Dufay, *Opera omnia,* ed. H. Besseler, V, Rome, 1966, p. xviii.]

MODERN EDITION: *Guillaume Dufay, *Sämtliche Hymnen,* ed. R. Gerber, Das Chorwerk, no. 49, Wolfenbüttel, 1937, pp. 6 f.

TRANSLATION:

Wicked Herod, why fearest thou Christ's coming?
He seeks no earthly kingdoms who grants heavenly ones.

The Magi come, following the star which guides the way; by its light they seek the Light; by their gifts they confess Him as God.

The heavenly Lamb touched the purifying fountain's waters; the sins, of which He was innocent, He cleansed us of, by His baptism.

A new sign of His power: the water jars redden and the water is poured out as wine, its substance transformed.

O Jesus, glory be to Thee who appeared to the nations
With the Father and the Holy Spirit for all eternity.   Amen.

PERFORMANCE SUGGESTIONS: ♩ = c. 80; also, see above.

Hostis Herodes

7 ⌇

ANONYMOUS (fifteenth century)

Ave rex angelorum

The carol is a particularly attractive and ingratiating genre of fifteenth-century English music. These anonymous pieces were used in various ways to adorn both liturgical and secular festive occasions, frequently serving as processional songs. Their origins still have not been fully explored, but apparently they go back to the earlier French *carole*, a sung, monophonic round dance. The tuneful and striking English carols, blending some of the complexities of art music with the popular style, provided musical settings that have a universal appeal. The narrative content and popular style of many of the texts also served to instruct the faithful. The majority of carols were for use during the Christmas season, two months long as celebrated then in England. But there were also Easter carols and May carols as well as those describing political or historic events, such as the famous Agincourt carol celebrating the great victory of Henry over the French in 1415.

The distinguishing feature of the English carol is its form, in which a refrain (called a burden), sung by the entire group, alternates with verses sung by soloists. Though some carols are monophonic, the writing is generally *a 2* and *a 3*, and the style ranges from very simple to quite complex and from tender or thoughtful to exuberant. *Ave rex angelorum*, an Epiphany carol, is typical of many composed in the serious rather than the popular vein. The text (only one verse survives), with its mixture of Latin and English, is also typical of many carols. The modification of the burden in its second appearance is not unusual.

The lovely and supple part writing in this carol makes an *a capella* performance mandatory. There should be a rich warmth in the vocal quality, with careful, expressive, and vivid shaping of the many eighth-note details. The two burdens should be sung by the full ensemble (twelve to twenty-four voices), with the verse between sung by three soloists. At the written pitch or a tone lower, the top line calls for tenors, with baritones on the other two parts. If transposed a minor third higher, the top line is suitable for countertenors or altos, with tenors on the other parts.

SOURCE: British Museum, Egerton Ms. 3307, fols. 55′–57.

MODERN EDITION: *Mediaeval Carols*, ed. J. Stevens, Musica Britannica, IV, rev. ed., London, 1958, pp. 40 f.

TRANSLATION (*Burdens*):
Hail, king of angels,
and Hail, king of the heavens,
and Hail, prince of the ends of the earth.

PERFORMANCE SUGGESTIONS: ♩ = c. 74; also, see above.

Ave rex angelorum

8 ∾

WALTER FRYE (fl. 1410)

Ave Regina coelorum

Three Masses, five motets, and four chansons are all that remain of the works of Walter Frye, one of the mid-fifteenth-century Englishmen working on the Continent. Though only one of his pieces survives in an English source, his compositions are generously represented in Burgundian manuscripts; for example, his *Ave Regina coelorum* appears in no less than thirteen different Burgundian sources. The three organ transcriptions of this piece in the *Buxheim Organ Book* are further proof that it was a great favorite in its time. The motet was also faithfully reproduced in two contemporary paintings, one of which shows the tenor part, and another both the discant and the tenor. Obrecht based a Mass and motet on the tenor part, indicating his own high regard for the piece.

The text of Frye's *Ave Regina* is not that of the well-known Marian antiphon (see the two following pieces), but is a Compline responsory then in use. As in the usual Burgundian style, the soprano and tenor form a self-sufficient two-voice structure, with the untexted contratenor sometimes filling the gap between these two parts and at other times dropping below to supply a bass. The ABCB form, unusual for its time, follows the repetition scheme of the text. The intimacy of this songlike piece, its relative simplicity and shortness, and its appropriateness for private devotions make it a perfect example of what modern scholars call a "song motet." It is, in short, much like a chanson and it is no accident that it was included in several *chansonniers*.

Solo voices are best for this gentle work, though it is also suitable for a small, light-sounding vocal ensemble. If desired, it can be performed twice, following one of two alternatives: (1) instrumentally, then repeated vocally (either solo voices or ensemble); or (2) with only the top voice sung (preferably solo), then repeated with both vocal parts sung (preferably by ensemble). The performance must have warmth, supple phrasing, and a lithe sense of rhythm.

SOURCE: Trent, Castello del Buon Consiglio, Cod. 90, fols. 298′–299.

MODERN EDITION: *Walter Frye, *Collected Works*, ed. S. Kenney, Rome, 1960, pp. 8 f.

TRANSLATION:

Hail, Queen of the heavens, mother of the King of angels,
O Mary, flower of virgins, even as the rose or lily.
Pour forth prayers to thy Son for the deliverance of the faithful.
O Mary, flower of virgins, even as the rose or lily.

PERFORMANCE SUGGESTIONS: ♩ = c. 82

    S.   countertenor or alto, or soprano if transposed a tone higher
    T.   tenor
    Ct.   bass viol
       or

S.   countertenor, alto, or soprano (transposed)
T.   tenor or bass viol
Ct.   bass viol or lute
        or
S.   tenor recorder (better a tone higher than at pitch)
T.   tenor or bass viol
Ct.   lute
        or
S.   alto recorder, or soprano recorder if transposed a tone higher
T.   treble viol (an octave higher)
Ct.   lute (an octave higher)

Ave Regina coelorum

Walter Frye

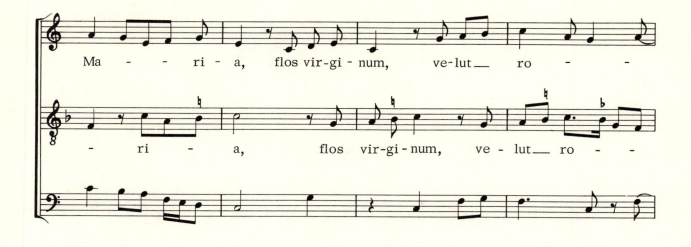

Ma - - ri - a, flos vir-gi - num, ve-lut__ ro - -

- - ri - a, flos vir-gi - num, ve - lut__ ro - -

- sa _____ ve-lut__ li - li - um:

sa _____ ve - lut _____ li-li - - um:

Fun - de pre - ces ad__ fi - li - um,

Fun - de__ pre - ces__ ad fi - li - um, Pro

Pro sa-lu - - - - - - te fi -
_____ sa - lu - - - te fi -

de - - - - li - um. O___
de - - - li - um. O Ma-

Ma - ri - a, flos vir - gi - num, ve-lut___ ro - -
- ri - a, flos vir-gi-num, ve-lut___ ro -

- sa_____ ve-lut___ li - li - um.
- sa ve - lut_____ li-li - um.

9 ⟋⟍

JOHANNES OCKEGHEM (c. 1420–c. 1495)

Alma Redemptoris Mater

The exquisite eleventh-century Lydian melody *Alma Redemptoris Mater* is the antiphon for the Blessed Virgin Mary sung in the daily Office from Advent to the Feast of the Purification. It was set polyphonically by all the leading early masters from Dunstable through Gombert, and served as the basis for several Masses. Most of Ockeghem's motets are settings of Marian texts, and the *Alma Redemptoris* is one of his most inspired works.

Because Ockeghem's sacred music is composed in a highly individual style, the underlying structure is often difficult to discern. In this motet, the alto part carries the chant melody, freely paraphrasing it as indicated in the score. Thus, each short phrase of the chant generates a corresponding, but much longer, phrase in the alto part. This part runs continuously throughout the entire piece, with rests of only one or two beats between the end of one phrase and the beginning of the next. The varying textural treatments of each of the alto phrases (such as the two contrasting opening duos and the four-voice writing that follows) fill out the shape and form of the piece. Further confirming the overall form are the cadences that occur at the ends of the alto phrases. To be sure, except in three instances (mm. 9, 41, and, of course, 52), Ockeghem deliberately bridges over these cadences with movement in at least one other part to avoid too obvious a stop or seam. Yet even though partially disguised, the cadences are there and serve as all-important clues to the structure.

The piece as a whole divides into two main sections. The first clearly ends at the full, four-voice cadence in measure 52, and the second begins in the next measure with a change of meter as well as a textural contrast. The overall two-part form is further articulated by the characteristic Ockeghem "drive to the cadence" in the concluding portions of both halves of the piece. This increasingly excited motion results from the use of fewer and fewer rests in the continuous four-part texture, along with the greater number of quicker notes. The long melisma at the end of the piece, on the penultimate syllable of the text paraphrases the opening of the chant and is given not to the alto as before, but to the top voice, making its presence absolutely unmistakable. This ingenious device gives the whole through-composed form an element of return.

A general characteristic of Ockeghem's music (like that of his great predecessor, Dufay) is the almost complete absence of imitation. Only occasional imitation occurs in the *Alma Redemptoris,* with short bits of the alto part appearing from time to time in the top line or in the bass. Harmonic ambiguity, another frequent trait of Ockeghem's music (see no. 2), is less pronounced in the *Alma,* since for the most part the harmonic framework is clear. However, the three Phrygian cadences (mm. 9, 19, and 34) and the many ornamental passing harmonies serve to enrich the bright clarity of the prevailing C major of the Ionian mode.

Perhaps the most obvious feature of Ockeghem's style, and the one that has caused the greatest difficulty in understanding and performing his music, is its highly individual contrapuntal texture. Long, soaring, surging or independently meandering melodic lines occur simultaneously in all the voices with seeming disregard for each other. Actually, here, as in any contrapuntal texture, each part creates a continuous cause-and-effect relationship with the other parts. It is only because of Ockeghem's fantastic and whimsical melodic shapes that the listener is struck more by the horizontal than the vertical relationships. A comparison of this motet with his Gloria (no. 2) will illustrate the range of Ockeghem's creativity; an examination of Dufay's setting of the same *Alma Redemptoris* text[1] will provide a fascinating comparison between the two styles.

This piece lies ideally for S.A.T.B. voices. Performance either with or without instruments will be totally convincing, though instrumental doubling may prove desirable simply for support. Although the alto part provides the entire scaffolding of the piece, it is in no way differentiated in style from the other voices; and therefore, in performance, it should not be set off from the other parts. (For a somewhat similar situation see no. 3, Obrecht's Credo of his *Missa Fortuna desperata*.) Each voice part must be given its many subtle nuances and accentuations independently of the others. To a certain extent, many of the largest dynamic shadings will result automatically from ascending-versus-descending lines as well as from the high or low tessitura of certain passages.[2] The many changes from two-voice to four-voice writing will also bring about dynamic contrasts. Regardless of all other factors, the performance should be imbued with a serene but glowing ardor.

This motet, like all chant-based pieces, was intended to replace in the liturgy the chant on which it was based. However, a very effective concert performance would include the singing of the chant before the motet.

SOURCES: Florence, Biblioteca Riccardiana 2794, fols. 11′–13; Rome, Sistine Chapel 46, fols. 115′–118.

MODERN EDITION: *Altniederländische Motetten,* ed. H. Besseler, Kassel, 1929, pp. 5 ff.

TRANSLATION:
Gracious mother of the Redeemer, who remains at the open portal of heaven, star of the sea, help thy fallen people who strive to rise. Thou who bore thy sacred Creator, while nature marveled, Virgin then as now, accepting that "ave" from Gabriel's lips, have pity on sinners.

PERFORMANCE SUGGESTIONS: ♩ = c. 68; at C, ♩ = 90; at $\frac{6}{4}$, ♩. = c. 45

NUMBER OF VOICES: twelve to thirty-six, with or without instruments.

S.	sopranos	with tenor recorder
A.	altos or countertenors	with bass recorder or portative organ
Ct.	tenors	with portative organ, or tenor or bass viol
T.	baritones/basses	with bass viol

MODERN SCORING:

S.	with flute
A.	with organ
Ct.	with viola
T.	with cello

---

[1] A. T. Davison and W. Apel, eds., *Historical Anthology of Music,* 2 vols., Cambridge, Mass., 1949, I, no. 65, pp. 70–71.

[2] For comments about dynamic nuances happening "automatically," see the Introduction, page 8.

Alma Redemptoris Mater

Al - - - - ma___ Re-dem-pto-ris___ Ma - ter,

quae per - vi - a___cae-li por - ta ma - nes, Et stel - la ma - ris,

suc - cur - re ca-den - - - ti sur-ge-re qui cu - rat___ po-pu-lo:

Tu___ quae ge-nu - i - sti,___ na - tu - ra mi-ran - - te,

tu - um___ san-ctum___ Ge - ni - to-rem: Vir - go pri - us

ac po - ste - ri - us, Ga-bri-e - lis ab___ o - re___

su-mens___ il - lud___ A - ve, pec-ca-to-rum___ mi-se-re - re.

10 ⚬∾

MARTIN DE RIVAFLECHA (d. 1528)

Salve, Regina

The golden age of the Catholic monarchs, Isabelle and Ferdinand, saw the first full flowering of native Spanish music. A large secular repertory appeared (see no. 26) as well as a considerable amount of sacred music, composed in the international Flemish style, yet bearing unmistakable signs of Spanish mysticism and fervor. Spanish sacred music was to reach its pinnacle within the century with Morales and Victoria.

Martin de Rivaflecha was chapelmaster at the cathedral of Valencia. None of his music was printed in his own lifetime, and only five pieces survive in a manuscript at the Biblioteca Columbina, that immense library in Seville founded by Christopher Columbus's son Ferdinand.

The *Salve, Regina,* one of the four antiphons in honor of the Blessed Virgin (see no. 9), is sung at Compline and Vespers during the last quarter of the church year. The Spanish had such a predilection for this antiphon that they sang it during other parts of the year as well, even at the conclusion of certain Masses. Consequently, many Spanish settings of this chant remain.

The Gregorian *Salve, Regina* was traditionally sung antiphonally by divided choir. Rivaflecha's setting, like those of many other Renaissance composers, retains this format by alternating chant with polyphonic sections which paraphrase those portions of the chant that they replace. As indicated in the score,[1] the paraphrase appears in the top voice of the first three sections and in

the tenor of the fourth section. The final part does not appear to have any connection with the chant. Since the four parts are present almost all the time, there is very little possibility for imitation; isolated examples occur only at "gementes et flentes," "lachrimarum," and "O clemens." The polyphonic style, though restrained, is highly effective in creating a sensitive texture with many subtle shifts of emphasis. The first four notes of the tenor part pervade the entire motet, contributing a unifying element to its through-composed form. The work is almost pure Dorian mode, faithful to the chant. The polish of the contrapuntal writing shows the influence of the Netherlands style, but the expressive simplicity of this music plus its special mixture of tenderness and austerity mark it as the work of a native Spaniard.

These qualities, and the long, beautifully shaped lines and the many subtle shifts of sonority, make an *a cappella* performance essential. The written pitch is ideal for countertenors (or altos), tenors, baritones, and basses, and the range of the chant portions makes them suitable for all voices except countertenors. Performance of this motet by S.A.T.B. is perfectly feasible a minor third higher. Although the general dynamic level should be relatively soft, the vocal quality must be intense and have a perfectly supported legato. The expressiveness of the lines must be brought out with gentle dynamic shadings. The tempo must be flexible and allowed to press forward a little or hold back in many places. The whole performance must catch the

---

[1] The notes of the chant melody are indicated in the score by small crosses.

quiet fervor of this piece, allowing the monophony of the beautiful chant antiphon and Riva- flecha's polyphony mutually to enhance each other.

SOURCE: *Seville, Biblioteca Capitular Columbina, Ms. 5-5-20, fols. 25'–27.

TRANSLATION:

Hail, O Queen, mother of mercy,
Our life, our sweetness, our hope.
To thee we cry, banished children of Eve;
To thee we send up our sighs, mourning and weeping in this vale of tears.
Turn then, our advocate, thine eyes of mercy toward us;
And after this our exile, show unto us the blessed fruit of thy womb, Jesus.
O clement, O loving, O ever-sweet Virgin Mary.[2]

PERFORMANCE SUGGESTIONS: ♩ = c. 72; also, see above.

---

[2] Rivaflelcha's text has two variants: the omission of "et" before "spes," and the addition of "semper" near the end.

Salve, Regina

Sal - ve, Re - gi - na,___ ma-ter mi - se - ri - cor-di - ae:

In moderately fast halves

S. Vi - ta dul -

A. Vi - ta___ dul - ce - - - -

T. Vi - ta dul - - ce -

B. Vi - ta___ dul - ce - -

- - ce - - - do Spes no -

- - - - do___ Spes no-stra___

- - - do Spes no -

- - - - do Spes___ no -

Martin de Rivaflecha

11

ANTOINE BRUMEL (c. 1460–c. 1520)

Mater patris et filia

Antoine Brumel's career took him to the cathedrals of Chartres, Laon, Notre Dame in Paris, and Lyons. Like so many of his contemporaries, he also worked in Italy. He served as *maestro di cappella* in Ferrara to Duke Alfonso I, successor to Hercules I, at whose brilliant court Obrecht, Ghiselin, and Josquin had served. Brumel's compositions include sixteen Masses, motets, and over fifty chansons.

The appealing, popular qualities of *Mater patris et filia* readily explain its inclusion in Petrucci's *Odhecaton*—basically a collection of chansons—and in Italian and German lute tablatures. Josquin based a parody Mass on it, and much later in the century, its opening phrase was used by both Lassus and Morley in their textless *bicinia*. The rhymed text, one of many that found their way into the liturgy during the early Renaissance and that remained in official use for a considerable time, was intended as a substitute for the usual Marian antiphon in the Saturday Office of the Virgin.[1]

Pervading imitation set off by the two short chordal passages illuminating the words "Audi nostra suspiria" and "Bone Jesu, Fili Dei" clearly articulates the through-composed form. The imitative sections are built on attractive and well-shaped motives, which are themselves contrasted in duos using ostinato (mm. 40–43) and canon (mm. 25–32). The change to triple meter for the closing section is quite common in motets of this period (see no. 9); but it is Brumel's masterful use of stretto, with its inevitable increase of intensity, that makes the final part of the prayer even more fervent. This last section is a fine example of the "drive to the cadence" so often found in the music of Ockeghem and his successors.

Mater patris uses to full advantage the particular sonorities possible with three male voices lying close together in the same range. *A cappella* performance is mandatory, with from nine to twenty-four performers. The voice parts lie perfectly for tenors I, tenors II, and baritones. Pliant phrasing and a warm vocal sound are essential to the performance of this lovely miniature.

SOURCE: *Harmonice musices Odhecaton A*, Petrucci, Venice, 1501, fols. 67'–68.
MODERN EDITION: *Josquin des Prez, *Werken*, ed. A. Smijers, *Missen*, III, Amsterdam, 1950, p. 29.

TRANSLATION:
Mother and Daughter of the Father, happiest of women, rarest star of the sea, hear our sighs; O Queen who attendest the heavens, Mother of mercy, in this vale of misery, grant us solace, O Mary, because of thy Son. O good Jesus, Son of God, hear our prayers. And to our entreaties grant us relief. Amen.

PERFORMANCE SUGGESTIONS: ♩ = c. 74; also, see above.

---

[1] As discovered by J. A. Mattfeld in her "Some Relationships between the Texts and *Cantus Firmi* in the Liturgical Motets of Josquin des Pres," *Journal of the American Musicological Society*, XIV (1961), 160 f., and especially n. 7.

Mater patris et filia

12 ❧

HEINRICH ISAAC (c. 1450–1517)

Gaudeamus omnes-Cum iocunditate

In 1508, the cathedral chapter at Constance commissioned Heinrich Isaac to undertake the enormous project of composing complete settings of the Proper of the Mass for the entire church year. The monumental collection that resulted, entitled *Choralis Constantinus,* is a milestone in the history of music. It comprises settings of the Propers for all Sundays as well as for certain feasts and saints' days, and concludes with five *alternatim* settings of the Ordinary (see no. 5). All of the pieces make use of the chant melodies then current at Constance. Though Isaac sometimes used the chant melodies as unadorned *cantus firmi,* far more often the chants are embellished so that they have the same melodic style as the other voice parts. At times in the cycle the chant melodies appear in more than one voice; at other times they are used imitatively. The great freedom and variety of Isaac's treatment of the chant shows the consummate skill and imagination with which he composed in the international Flemish style. The collection, not quite finished when he died, was completed by his pupil, Ludwig Senfl.

Gaudeamus omnes is the Introit from the Mass for the Feast of Our Lady of Mount Carmel.[1] All Introits have the ABA form of antiphon—Psalm verse—antiphon repeated. Isaac consistently sets the antiphon polyphonically, then follows with the first half of the Psalm verse sung in chant, and the second half set polyphonically. The *Gloria Patri,* which always concludes the Psalm verse, is left in chant, and the opening antiphon

setting is then repeated. Thus all the Introits, laid out in this *alternatim* arrangement, follow the same ground plan of polyphony—chant—polyphony—chant—polyphony, providing a perfect example of the aesthetically pleasing result typical of *alternatim* pieces.

Simultaneous with the chant melody of the present Introit, Isaac uses the text and chant of the Vespers antiphon *Cum iocunditate.*[2] The two chant melodies are paraphrased as follows: in the opening antiphon, *Gaudeamus* is in the highest voice, while the shorter *Cum iocunditate* appears first in the alto voice and is then repeated almost identically in the bass, beginning in measure 22. For the second half of the Psalm verse, Isaac paraphrases the Gregorian psalm tone in the tenor. The brief silences in the upper voices now call attention to this voice, thereby nicely balancing the tenor's earlier lack of any share in the chant melody. The tenor paraphrase is answered canonically by the highest voice, contrasting the treatment of this section of the movement with the nonimitative polyphony of the antiphon. The appropriate Gregorian psalm tone for the *Gloria Patri* completes the B section of the Introit, after which the opening antiphon is repeated.

The extraordinary degree of independence in the part writing is typical of much of Isaac's music. Equally striking is the strong harmonic feel-

[1] *Liber Usualis,* Tournai, 1963, p. 1556. The chant is included here for comparison with Isaac's setting.

[2] *Ibid.,* p. 1626. This is one of the antiphons from Second Vespers for the Feast of the Nativity of the Blessed Virgin Mary. The chant is included here for comparison with Isaac's setting.

ing fostered by the frequent clear cadences on the principal tonal degrees of the scale (B flat, C, D, G).

Gaudeamus omnes is ideal for soprano, alto (or countertenor), tenor, and bass voices, with the chant portions sung by tenors and countertenors. The opening intonation should be sung by a solo voice. This piece is most effectively performed by a relatively large group of singers doubled by loud winds, as suggested below. A bright, rich vocal sound is ideal. Since the voice parts carrying the paraphrase have the same melodic style as the other parts, they must not be given any added prominence. The performance must pay special attention to the above-mentioned independent part writing and the constant flow of ever-new melodic motives. A very effective heightening of the large ABA form is achieved by performing the Psalm verse (mm. 55–70) *a cappella.*

SOURCE: Heinrich Isaac, *Tomus Secundus. Choralis Constantinus,* Formschneider, Nuremberg, 1555.

MODERN EDITION: **Choralis Constantinus,* Book II, ed. A. von Webern, *Denkmäler der Tonkunst in Österreich,* Jahrg. XVI[1], Band 32, pp. 134 f.

TRANSLATION:

Gaudeamus omnes: Let us all rejoice in the Lord, keeping a feast day in honor of the Blessed Virgin Mary, for whose celebration the angels rejoice and unite in praising the Son of God.

My heart hath uttered a good word: I speak my words to the King. (Ps. 44:2)

Glory be to the Father and to the Son and to the Holy Ghost. As it was in the beginning, is now, and ever shall be, world without end. Amen.

Cum iocunditate: With joy, let us celebrate the nativity of Holy Mary, that she may intercede for us unto Jesus Christ, Son of God.

PERFORMANCE SUGGESTIONS: $\downarrow$ = c. 72

NUMBER OF VOICES: twenty to thirty-six.

S.	sopranos	with cornetto
A.	countertenors or altos	with alto shawm
T.	tenors	with tenor sackbut
B.	basses	with bass sackbut

Chant: tenors (and countertenors)

MODERN SCORING:

S.	with oboe
A.	with English horn
T.	with trombone
B.	with trombone

Gaudeamus omnes–Cum iocunditate

Fine

(*106*)   Heinrich Isaac

Introit D.C. al Fine

Cum ju - cun - di - ta - te Na - ti - vi - ta - tem be - a - tae

Ma - ri - ae ce - le - bre - mus, ut ip - sa pro no - bis

in - ter - ce - dat ad Do - mi - num Je - sum Chri - stum.

Gau - de - a - mus o - mnes in Do - mi - no,

di - em fe - stum ce - le - bran - tes sub ho - no - re

Ma - ri - ae Vir - gi - nis: de cu - jus sol - e - mni - ta - te gau - dent

An - ge - li, et col - lau - dant Fi - li - um De - i.

Psalm Verse

E - ru - cta - vit cor me - um ver - bum bo - num:

di - co e - go o - pe - ra me - a re - gi.

13 &

JOSQUIN DES PREZ (c. 1445–1521)

Jubilate Deo, omnis terra

The eighty-two motets by Josquin that survive include settings of an amazing variety of texts: Mass Propers, Psalms, antiphons, Marian texts, prayer and Gospel texts, hymns, David laments, and even settings of Virgil. Not only does this vast range include every textual form and liturgical function, but it also spans the entire gamut of emotion, from the greatest joy to the most profound despair and grief. If some of his Mass settings seem to show Josquin as a conservative, the enormous variety of motet texts stimulated his imagination to its fullest, inspiring him to an astonishing range of compositional techniques and much of his greatest music.

Although not the first composer to turn to the Psalms, Josquin established the Psalm-motet genre, leaving some twenty-five examples. This Psalm of praise (Ps. 99) is composed as a free setting without reference to any psalmodic chant formula. Its style is clearly that of Josquin's mature years, with a great variety of sonorous and textural interplay and notably vigorous declamation, such as the top voice's "Introite" in measures 27–31, and the bass's "veritas" in measures 109–112. Each phrase of the Psalm is given a new melodic idea, and the opening of each line is clarified by change of texture and density. The initial verbs are projected with crisp rhetorical rhythm ("Jubilate," "servite," "Introite," "Scitote"), and contrasting melismatic treatment is reserved for the close of the vibrant duos on "terra" and "laetitia" and for the end of the first part. While the opening pages of the motet shift from paired duos to trios and *tutti* sections, the full sonority is generally kept from verse 3 (m. 44) on. Considerable excitement is generated by one of Josquin's favored ostinato passages in syncopation (mm. 45–64), reaching a climax with the consolidation of all the parts on "confitemini." The second part, the setting of the fourth verse (mm. 72–124), uses a four-voice texture throughout, and affords a broad conclusion to the work. Imitation, a fundamental element in so much of Josquin's music (as it is in the first part of this motet) is entirely absent from this section.

This motet calls for a relatively large choir of countertenors (or altos), tenors, baritones, and basses, best doubled by loud winds. Transposition a minor third higher makes the piece perfectly suitable for S.A.T.B.

SOURCE: *Tomus secundus Psalmorum selectorum . . .* , J. Petreius, Nuremberg, 1539.
MODERN EDITION: *Josquin des Prez, *Werken*, ed. A. Smijers, *Motetten*, IV, Amsterdam, 1963, pp. 41 ff.

TRANSLATION:
> O be joyful in the Lord, all ye lands: serve the Lord with gladness, and come before His presence with a song.

> Be ye sure that the Lord He is God; it is He that hath made us and not we ourselves.

We are His people, and the sheep of His pasture:
O go your way into His gates with thanksgiving, and into His courts with praise, be thankful unto Him.

Speak good of His name, for the Lord is gracious, His mercy is everlasting, and His truth endureth from generation to generation.

PERFORMANCE SUGGESTIONS: $\downarrow$ = c. 72

NUMBER OF VOICES: twenty to thirty-six.

I—*At written pitch:*

S.	countertenors (or altos)	with alto shawm
A.	tenors	with tenor shawm
T.	baritones	with tenor sackbut
B.	basses	with bass sackbut

II—*A minor third higher:*

S.	sopranos	with treble shawm
A.	altos	with alto shawm
T.	tenors	with tenor sackbut
B.	basses	with bass sackbut

MODERN SCORING: Substitute oboe for treble shawm, English horn for alto shawm, bassoon for tenor shawm, and trombones for sackbuts.

Jubilate Deo, omnis terra

Josquin des Prez

14

JOSQUIN DES PREZ (c. 1445–1521)

Absalon fili mi

The Old Testament account of David lamenting the death of his beloved son Absalom was a favorite text with Renaissance composers. This powerful and moving setting by Josquin reveals yet another facet of the master's enormous range and imagination in responding to the meaning of whatever text he has chosen to set. One is, of course, immediately struck by the dark sonorities and very low range—going to the extreme with the final low B flat in the bass. The complete flexibility with which Josquin moves from imitative writing to free polyphony and back again with never the slightest seam, continuously building the most tightly integrated through-composed form, shows the dazzling contrapuntal skill of this composer. But it is the extraordinary harmonic and tonal arrangement of this piece, together with the most subtle use of dissonance, that makes this such an effective work, and confirms Josquin's place among the greatest composers of all time.

The numerous cadences on B flat and E flat plus the two tonicizations of F are in themselves not in the least unusual in Josquin's works. But the sudden darkening of the entire harmonic color by the appearance of the D-flat harmony in measure 52 on the word "Non" of "Non vivam ultra" is altogether striking. (The effect of this is all the more heightened by the facts that the bass, which has the D flat, enters with it after a rest, and that this is the bass part's lowest note thus far.)The same word is given a similar harmonic darkening by the fully sustained B-flat-minor harmony in measure 56. But the final circle-of-fifths progression on the words "sed descendam in infernum plorans" plumbs the depths

in its descent to the remote G-flat harmony just before the final cadence. There is a frequent use of a 6–5 progression, as in measures 38, 49, and 58, which simultaneously gives an added expressiveness to the line and enriches the harmonic movement, serving somewhat the same purpose as the appoggiatura does in later music. The fact that the harmonic motion occurs at least every two beats—and frequently on every beat—contributes much to the intense, restless quality of the piece. In order to allow the harmonic and tonal elements the fullest impact, Josquin ornaments the voice parts very little.

Because of the extreme range of the bass part, very few choral groups will find it possible to perform this work at its written pitch. For most groups it will have to be transposed at least a whole tone higher. However, regardless of the pitch used, if the voices remain in the lower part of their ranges, the dark color can be kept intact, even without benefit of the very low sonorities. The fact that two of the sources of this work contain a set of clefs suitable for high voices makes an upward transposition all the more valid, and brings the piece within S.A.T.B. range. The extreme low range of the second voice in measures 46–49 will almost certainly make it necessary for the two middle voices to exchange parts in measure 44, changing back in measure 50.

If one assumes a slow tempo for this piece, and adopts a dynamic range that never exceeds *mezzo forte* (and that may at times drop to *pianissimo* at moments like m. 73), it becomes especially important to maintain an intense vocal color. A sensitive shaping of phrases goes without saying, especially in staggered passages like "sed descendam." One may (and probably should) make at least subtle differences between the two statements of the final section. *A cappella* performance is strongly recommended.

SOURCE: *British Museum Royal Ms. 8 G VII, fols. 56'–58 (no attribution).

MODERN EDITION: Josquin des Prez, *Werken,* ed. A. Smijers, *Supplement,* eds. M. Antonowycz and W. Elders, Amsterdam, 1969, pp. 22 ff.

TRANSLATION:

Absalom, my son! my son, Absalom!
Would that I had died for you!
Let me live no longer,
But let me descend to hell, weeping!

PERFORMANCE SUGGESTIONS: ♩ = c. 56

NUMBER OF VOICES: twelve to thirty-two.

I—*At written pitch to a third higher:*

S. countertenors or altos
A. tenors
T. baritones
B. basses

II—*A fourth or fifth higher:*

S. sopranos
A. altos
T. tenors
B. basses

Absalon fili mi

Josquin des Prez

15 ∽

JEAN MOUTON (c. 1459–1522)

Noe, noe, psallite

Jean Mouton, colleague of Josquin and teacher of Willaert, held posts at Amiens Cathedral, Grenoble, and later Paris at the royal chapels of Louis XII and Francis I. Like Josquin, he became a canon at St. Quentin, where he died in 1522. Among his compositions are nine Masses and about seventy-five motets, but only a handful of secular pieces.

The lively Christmas motet *Noe, noe, psallite noe,* on which Arcadelt based a Mass, is a fine example of Mouton's work. It combines what the sixteenth-century theorist Glareanus called "melody flowing in a supple thread" with skillful and imaginative contrapuntal handling. Short, clearly shaped motives, with crisp rhythms generated by the words, are developed successively in points of imitation. Several different treatments are given to the key word "noe." Es-

pecially notable among these are the recurring duos which provide a kind of refrain within the otherwise through-composed form. Instances of pictorial setting—for example, the rising melodic lines at "fulget in caelo" and at "et elevamini, portae aeternales"—foreshadow the mid-century's "madrigalisms."

The vocal ranges lie perfectly for performance by soprano, alto (or counter-tenor), tenor, and bass. The light, agile qualities of this charming piece make it best suited for *a cappella* performance by a small vocal ensemble of twelve to twenty voices; four solo voices are also suitable. The performance must have a bright and almost playful joyousness. In order to have the rhythms sound very much alive, with the eighth-note figures clear and sparkling, all eighth notes should be somewhat detached or separately pulsed.

SOURCE: *Liber secundus: 24 musicales quatuor vocum Motetes . . .* , Attaingnant, Paris, 1534.

MODERN EDITION: **Treize livres de motets parus chez Pierre Attaingnant en 1534 et 1535,* ed. A. Smijers, Paris, 1936, II, pp. 86 ff.

TRANSLATION:
Noel, noel, sing (with instruments) noel.
Jerusalem, rejoice and be happy,
Because today the Savior of the world was born.
He lies in a manger; He shines in the sky.
Lift up your gates, O ye princes,
And be ye lifted up, O eternal gates;
And the King of Glory shall enter in.
Who is this King of Glory?
The Lord of hosts; He is the King of Glory.

PERFORMANCE SUGGESTIONS: ♩ = c. 84; also, see above.

Noe, noe, psallite

Jean Mouton

BARTOLOMEO TROMBONCINO (d. c. 1535)

Ave Maria

Bartolomeo Tromboncino, one of the most gifted among the new group of native-born Italian composers at the beginning of the sixteenth century, was long in the employ of Isabella d'Este's court at Mantua, and had much to do with Mantua's becoming one of the brilliant new centers of music (see no. 24). His music, in demand everywhere, was performed at the dazzling festivities for the wedding of Lucrezia Borgia, daughter of Pope Alexander VI, to Isabella's brother Alfonso d'Este. Tromboncino's unusually violent temper frequently got him into trouble —to the point of eventually murdering his unfaithful wife and her lover. But he was so highly regarded as a composer that, in time, he was cleared. He died about 1535. Though he is best known as one of the leading *frottola* composers of the time, he also wrote a number of *laude*.

Laude, vernacular devotional songs intended for laymen, had a long history dating back to St. Francis of Assisi and the many penitential fraternities. At that time the songs were monophonic and, to a certain extent, influenced by French troubadour music. The singing of these songs was the principal feature of the unofficial devotional services regularly held by the laymen societies called *laudesi.* Around the turn of the sixteenth century, several of the new Italian-born generation of *frottola* composers turned their attention also to *laude,* composing them now in much the same style as the *frottola* (see nos. 24 and 25). The first printed collection of *laude* is

contained in two volumes printed by Petrucci in 1507 and 1508, the second volume of which includes Tromboncino's *Ave Maria.*

This simple, devout piece has its main melody in the top voice, moving in short phrases punctuated by *fermatas* or rests. The other voices, though having some polyphonic independence, essentially provide a harmonic support. The tonal plan, however, is a curious mixture of the new Italian style, with its "modern" treatment of tonality (see no. 24), and the much older Phrygian mode (mm. 13–17, 52–end). The resulting harmonic ambiguity is both curious and appealing, and gives the piece a kind of improvised quality.

This gentle piece is best performed *a cappella,* though instrumental doubling is perfectly possible. At the written pitch, the voice parts are suitable for S.A.T.B. Because of the three places where the alto part drops too low for alto voices, it will be necessary to exchange alto and tenor parts (mm. 13–17, 29–33, and 47–55). Transposition down a minor third will make the piece suitable for countertenor (or alto), tenor, tenor, bass. If instruments are used, viols or organ would be appropriate. Tenor or bass recorder, or tenor Renaissance flute, doubling the top line, will give that part an added warmth and fulness. The qualities most essential for a good performance are a gentle, sensitive phrasing and a warm vocal sound.

SOURCE: *Laude, Libro secondo,* Petrucci, Venice, 1508, fols. 39'–40.
MODERN EDITION: **Die mehrstimmige italienische Laude um 1500,* ed. K. Jeppesen, Leipzig, 1935, pp. 64 f.

TRANSLATION:

Hail Mary, full of grace, the Lord is with thee.
Blessed are thou among women and blessed is the fruit of thy womb, Jesus.
Holy Mary, Mother of God, pray for us sinners,
Now and in the hour of our death.
Amen.

PERFORMANCE SUGGESTIONS: ♩ = c. 60

NUMBER OF VOICES: twelve to thirty-six, preferably without instrumental doubling.

I—*At written pitch:*

S.	sopranos	with treble or tenor viol, or tenor or bass recorder
A.	altos	with tenor viol
T.	tenors	with tenor or bass viol
B.	basses	with bass viol
		or
		organ

II—*A minor third lower:*

S.	countertenors	viols, if used, similar to the above
A.	tenors	*or*
T.	tenors/baritones	organ
B.	basses	

MODERN SCORING:

S.	with flute
A.	with viola
T.	with viola
B.	with cello

Ave Maria

Bartolomeo Tromboncino

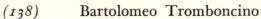

ne - di - ctus   fru - ctus   ven - tris   tu – i,   Je – sus.

San – – cta   Ma – ri – a,   ma – ter

De – i,   o – ra pro

17 ∾

HEINRICH FINCK (c. 1445–1527)

Christ ist erstanden

The pre-Reformation German composer Heinrich Finck was born about 1445 at Bamberg, and was as widely traveled as many of his great Flemish contemporaries. His career lay in the eastern European countries, however, rather than along the Flemish-Italian axis. He worked at the Polish court at Kraków, in Stuttgart, and in Salzburg (where he was *Kapellmeister* at the cathedral), and spent his last years as music director at the imperial court in Vienna, where he died in 1527.

His sacred and secular music (including Masses, motets, and many lieder) is in some ways very typical of the contemporary German idiom. Evolving by and large separately from the western tradition, German music had developed a more conservative style, in which the somewhat homophonic texture, rhythmic uniformity, and frequent cadential divisions were very different from the continuous linearity of the Franco-Netherlandish school. The influence of the Burgundians first found its way eastward through the works of the Dufay generation (see no. 28), but the most powerful westernizing force was the music of Isaac. The integration of Flemish free-flowing linearity with German clarity of tonality and structure paved the way for the momentous developments of the next two centuries of German music.

In *Christ ist erstanden*, Finck has woven together two Easter *leisen*, the traditional German folk hymns whose stanzas end with the refrain "Kyrieleis." [1] Though the simultaneous manipulation of two different tunes perhaps betrays the Flemish influence, the piece is nevertheless

clearly German: the tonal focus on G minor is stubborn, almost unmoving, without the overlapping cadences that help to give Flemish polyphony its subtle flexibility; the rhythmic patterns are clear and regular; the phrases are short; and the two tunes (*Christ ist erstanden* and *Christ der ist erstanden*) are assigned intact only to tenor and bass. Nevertheless, some contrapuntal complexities are present. The two top parts and the *vagans* offer occasional imitative comment on the two tunes, and the melodies themselves overlap in several places; in measures 45–53, for example, Finck restates part of the first *leise* simultaneously with a complete statement of the second. And, as though impatient to hear both melodies, the top voice sounds the opening phrase of the second *leise* (together with the first in the tenor) at the very outset.

A bright, solid vocal sound is best for this piece, with the two *leisen* standing out slightly in the contrapuntal texture. This can be accomplished to some extent with dynamics, but must be achieved more through contrast of timbres. Two approaches are possible, both outlined below; in both cases, the tenor and bass are to be sung and doubled instrumentally, with the other parts either sung only or played only. If all parts are to be sung, the alto line lies satisfactorily for countertenors or tenors, but is too low for altos; however, a few tenors singing with altos should largely solve this problem. An upward transposition, which solves problems of vocal range in many pieces, will not work in this case, since it would create (at least for most choral groups) new problems for the tenor and *vagans* parts.

---

[1] Also "Kyrioleis," "Kirleis," and "Leis."

SOURCE: *Schöne auserlesene Lieder des hochberühmten Heinrich Finckens,* Formschneider, Nuremberg, 1536.

MODERN EDITION: **Publikationen älterer praktischer und theoretischer Musikwerke,* ed. R. Eitner, Leipzig, 1879; Jahrg. VIII, pp. 1 ff.

TRANSLATION:

Christ has arisen from all his sufferings. Therefore we shall all rejoice, Christ will be our consolation. Kyrieleison.

PERFORMANCE SUGGESTIONS: $\downharpoonright$ = c. 84

NUMBER OF VOICES: four to eight on each part.

    S. cornetto
    A. tenor sackbut
    T. tenors with alto shawm (or tenor sackbut)
    V. tenor shawm (or tenor sackbut)
    B. basses with bass sackbut
      or
    S. sopranos
    A. countertenors, tenors, or altos and tenors
    T. tenors with tenor sackbut or alto shawm
    V. baritones
    B. basses with bass sackbut

MODERN SCORING: oboe in place of cornetto, English horn in place of·alto shawm, trombones in place of sackbuts and tenor shawm.

Christ ist erstanden

1. **Choir** singing from the Graduale. Woodcut detail from Hans Weiditz's *Emperor Maximilian at Mass*.

2. Facsimile pages of Rivaflecha's *Salve, Regina*. Seville, Biblioteca Colombina, Ms. 5-5-20, folios 25'–27.

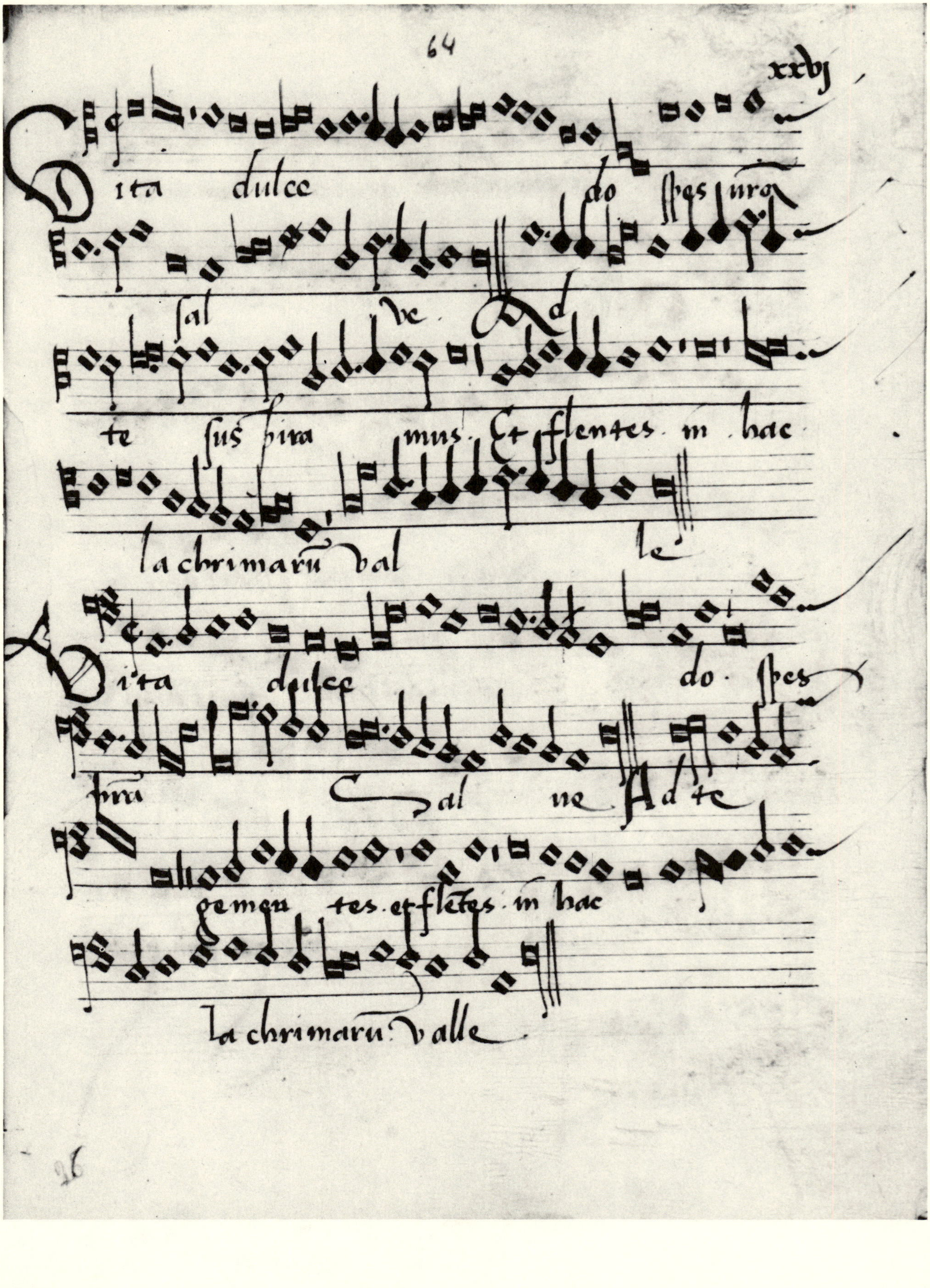
64
xxvj
ita dulce do spes nra
sal ue. Ad
te sus pira mus. Et flentes in hac
lachrimaru val le
ita dulce do spes
nra Sal ue Ad te
gemen tes. et fletes in hac
lachrimaru valle

65
xxvij
Jhm beedictum fru
ctum ventris tui O cle
men O Dul
cis virgo semper Mari a
Jhm Benedictum fructum
ventris tui O clemens
O dul
cis
virgo semp maria

3. *The Death of Absalom.* Woodcut from *Das Ander teyl des alten testaments* . . . Wittenberg, Melchior Lottes, 1524.

4. Albrecht Dürer, *Courtyard at Innsbruck.* Water color.

5. Filarete, *Pope Eugene IV Crowning Sigismund, Holy Roman Emperor*. Detail from one of St. Peter's Doors, Rome.

6. *Positive-Organ Player and Tuning Lutenist*. Woodcut from the Malermi Bible, Venice, 1490.

7. *A Wedding Couple Dancing to the Lute*. Woodcut from an edition of *Aesop's Fables* printed in Naples, 1485.

8. Facsimile pages of Josquin's *Absalon fili mi*. British Museum, Royal MS 8 G VII, folios 56′–58.

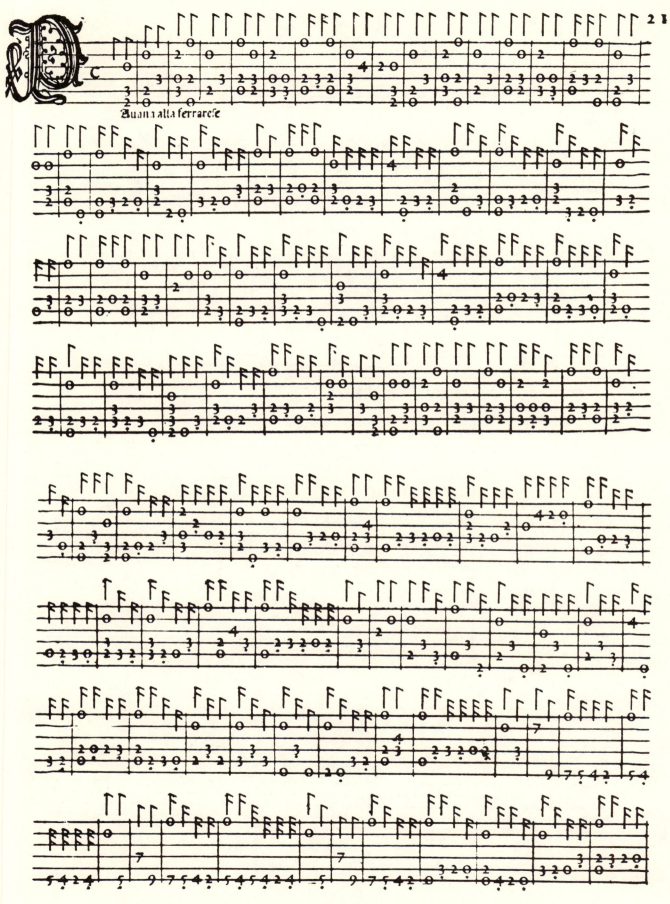

21

9. Facsimile pages of the *Pavana alla ferrarese,* from Dalza's *Intabulatura de Lauto* . . .
Venice, Petrucci, 1508.

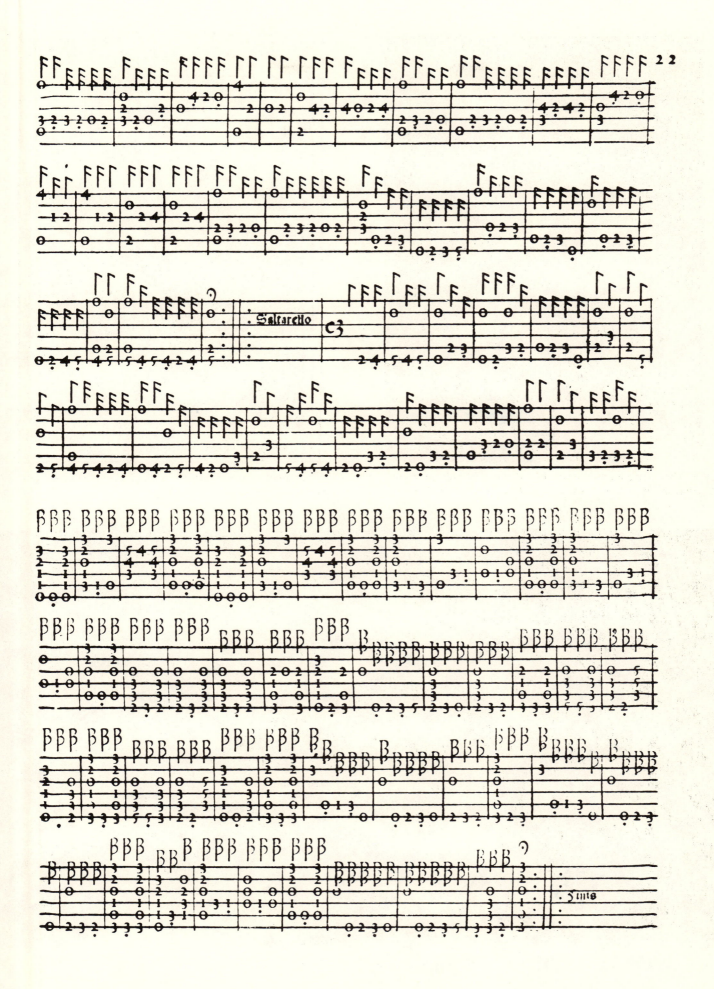

10. Michelangelo, *Lorenzo de' Medici*. Detail from the sculpture in the sacristy of the Church of San Lorenzo, Florence.

11. *Student Drinking Bout*. Woodcut from Directorium Statuu, Strasbourg, 1489.

12. Paolo Uccello, battle scene from *La battaglia di S. Egidio.*

Qui totum noſtris ſubdent quoq; legibus orbẽ:
  Maxima qua tellus:qua freta lata patent.
Poſt ubi proſcindent fatalia ſtamina parcæ:
  Scandet in æthereas lætus uterq; domos.

Impreſſum Romæ per Magiſtrum Eucha
rium Silber : alias Franck: Anno Domini
M.CCCC.XCIII.Die uero.VII.Martii.

                    Regiſtrum.
Primum uacat   Et Africa
  ſtrorum tempoꝶ   ta Granata
Conuocandi.   Marcellini
  potentiæ ac   Attamen
Munitum
  metum hoſti

Viua el gran Re Don Fernando
  Con la Reyna Don Iſabella
  Viua ſpagna e la Caſtella
  Pien de gloria triumphando
La Cita Mahomectana Potentiſſima Granata.
  Da la falſa ſe pagana E diſſolta e liberata
  Per uirtute & manu armata.Del Fernãdo e Li
ſabella.   Viua ſpagna &c:.

13. Facsimile pages of *Viv' el gran Re Don Fernando*.
Music on the following page printed from wood blocks,
in Carlo Verardi's *Historia baetica,* Rome, 1493.

Gran auſpicio e gran impreſa
Gran conſiglio e gran uirtute
Gran honore a ſancta chieſa
A ignoranti gran ſalute
Gran prouincia in ſeruitute
Al Fernando & Liſabella.   Viua ſpagna zc.

Noſtra ſede ciaſchun ſenti
Quanto a queſti e obligata
Per che Mori non contenti
Daſia & Africa occupata
In Europa debacchata
Gia faccuan ſforzo & uela.   Viua ſpagna zc.

Hora ognun fa feſta e canti
El ſignor regratiando
Per tal palma tucti quanti
Dirren ben forte gridando
Viua el gran Re don Fernando
Colla Reina don Iſabella.
              Viua Spagna e la Caſtella
              Pien de gloria triumphando.

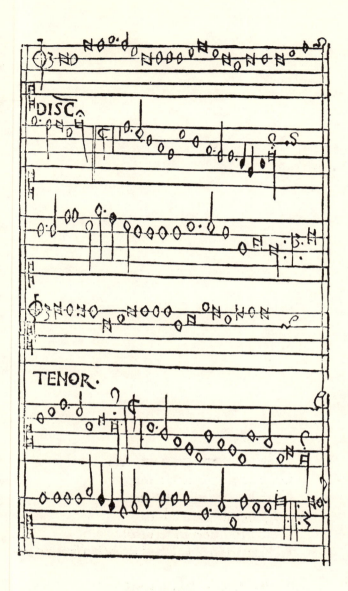

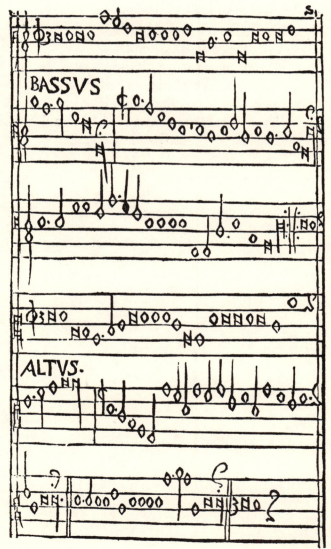

18 ∽

LUDWIG SENFL(?) (c. 1490–c. 1556)
Da Jakob nu das Kleid ansah

Those parts of German-speaking countries that remained Catholic after the Reformation produced very few outstanding native composers during the sixteenth century. The notable exception is Ludwig Senfl. Born in Zurich around 1490, he sang in the court choir of Maximilian I and was the most illustrious pupil of Heinrich Isaac. He served as court composer during Isaac's absences, and was appointed official composer himself after Isaac's death in 1517. After Maximilian's death in 1519, Senfl was appointed to a similar position at the Bavarian court at Munich. Like Isaac before him and Lassus after, Senfl became in his day the most gifted exponent of the Netherlands tradition in German countries.

His works include seven Masses, numerous motets, and over 250 lieder. Among the latter are some of the finest examples of German songs of the sixteenth century, ranging from the most exuberantly obscene to the most poignant and profound.

Da Jakob nu das Kleid ansah first appeared in a large collection printed in 1544 by George Rhaw, then the leading publisher of music for the Lutheran church. Except for Senfl's piece and a few others, the rest of the collection consisted of music by Protestant composers. *Da Jakob* is one of Senfl's sacred songs, a devotional but non-liturgical piece set to a free, rhymed paraphrase of Genesis 37:33–35, which tells of Jacob's grief over the presumed death of his favorite son Joseph. Everything about this exceptionally moving composition indicates total mastery of the Josquin legacy: the thoroughly vocal conception, the striking and dramatic contrasts between continuous, overlapping imitation and declamatory chordal style, and the two duos. But these alone hardly explain the particular radiance of the work. More germane are such elements as the warm sonority of moderately low and close scoring, the strong harmonic impact (even some of the points of imitation produce sustained triads), and the tight cohesiveness derived from the opening measures of the bass, whose ascending third and subsequent descent permeates so much of the piece. The expressive treatment of words like "Schmerzen" and "Leide" and the heightened emotion of the words "O Joseph" achieved by the brief F-major passage set against the prevailing Dorian tonic are prophetic of the musical era soon to come.

There is some evidence that this piece may have been composed by a minor compatriot of Senfl's, Cosmas Alder. But its high artistic quality would seem to support Senfl as its creator.

Performance should be by *a cappella* choir or four solo voices. A warm, glowing vocal sound, shapely and expressive phrasing, and a subtle flexibility of tempo will allow the tragic qualities of this piece to be heard to their fullest.

SOURCE: *Newe deudsche geistliche Gesange für die gemeinen Schulen . . .*, Rhaw, Wittenberg, 1544.
MODERN EDITION: **Denkmäler deutscher Tonkunst*, ed. J. Wolf, Band 34, p. 180.

TRANSLATION:

When Jacob saw the coat, he spoke with great pain: "Alas, the great woe, my dear son is dead; wild beasts have torn him apart and have rent him with their teeth. O Joseph, Joseph, my dear son! Who will now comfort me in my old age? For I must die of grief and sadly go from this earth.

PERFORMANCE SUGGESTIONS: ♩ = c. 54; also, see above.

Da Jakob nu das Kleid ansah

(150)   Ludwig Senfl (?)

O Jo-seph, Jo-seph,___ mein lie - ber___ Sohn, Wer will mich Al - - - ten trö - sten nun?

O Jo-seph, Jo - seph, Jo - seph, mein lie - - ber Sohn,___ mein lie - ber Sohn, Wer will mich Al - - ten trö - sten nun? Denn

O Jo - seph, Jo - seph,___ mein lie - ber Sohn, Wer will mich Al - ten, wer will mich Al - ten trö - - - sten nun?

O Jo-seph, Jo - - seph,___ mein lie - ber Sohn,___ wer will mich Al - ten er-freu-en nun? Denn ich vor

Ludwig Senfl (?)

PART III ∾

SECULAR VOCAL MUSIC

Sacred compositions represented only a portion of the vast treasure of fifteenth- and sixteenth-century vocal music. The cultivated Renaissance aristocrat, well versed in singing and playing, sought every opportunity to display his skill in ensemble as well as in solo music. Composers working at the courts of Burgundy, France, and Italy were constantly besieged for new music that would be suitable for domestic festivities as well as court entertainments; they replied with a plentiful and varied supply of secular vocal pieces.

These pieces ranged from the graceful elegance of Dufay's chansons and the intensely emotional ones of Ockeghem to the brilliantly varied settings of Josquin, all in the northern linear style.

At the same time, the new native styles, influenced by the folk traditions of the various countries, were producing simpler and more tuneful pieces, with less complex rhythms and textures and clearer tonal structures. Many of these pieces were actual settings of folk songs. Among the characteristically differing national genres that emerged were the Italian *frottola,* the Spanish *villancico,* the German lied, the English part song, and the "new" French chanson. The interaction of this new secular style with the continuing Flemish polyphonic idiom sparked the long and glorious development of the madrigal, destined to reach its brilliant climax a century later.

19

GUILLAUME DUFAY(?) (c. 1400–1474)

Je ne vis oncques la pareille

The chanson enjoyed its first full flowering in the fifteenth century with the Burgundians Dufay and Binchois, soon followed by Ockeghem and Busnois. Their chansons, usually with French texts, survive in large numbers in the beautifully decorated manuscript collections known as *chansonniers*. These contain May songs, New Year songs, and drinking songs; but by far the favorite subject was love. Unrequited love gave the poet cause to complain and to view life with a gentle melancholy and resignation. True to the convention of the courtly poetry of the preceding century, the poet's lady was held at arm's length, so that his greatest joy lay in singing of her beauty and honor and vowing his lifelong faithfulness. The style of the chanson—both text and music—changed several times during the course of the succeeding decades (see no. 22), and some of the later texts were anything but courtly. Still, the chanson, retaining a central position throughout the entire period, was to the Renaissance what the art song later became to the nineteenth century.

Among Dufay's fifty-nine chansons, the most commonly found form is the rondeau, one of the *formes fixes* of late medieval French poetry and music that survived into the early fifteenth century. For each of these fixed forms, the poetry followed a prescribed and rigid structural plan; musical settings of these forms followed the poetic structure exactly. Thus, judging from the music alone, the rondeau appears to be a short piece in AB form;[1] but in fact, the musical form is ABAAABAB, the repetitions caused by the repeat structure of the poem. Five lines of poetry are expanded into an eight-line structure, with music supplied only for the first two lines. The rondeau may be diagramed as follows:

| music: | A B A A A B A B |
| line of poem: | 1 2 3 1 4 5 1 2 |

(Only the first two lines of *Je ne vis oncques* are given with the music; the complete text is supplied below.)

Almost all of the Burgundian chansons are written *a 3:* soprano, tenor, and contratenor. (For a discussion of the compositional arrangements of these parts, see no. 6.) The top voice, carrying the main melody, naturally had the text; the tenor was very often texted as well; the contratenor, a more or less "filling in" part, rarely had text, and presumably was intended for an instrument. The melodic style of *Je ne vis oncques*[2] is typical of Dufay's finest writing. The contours of the long phrases are beautifully shaped; the many small details within them are supple and irregular. An unusual feature of *Je ne vis oncques*, for its time, is that the contratenor lies almost consistently below the tenor instead of crisscrossing it in the same range, and functions as an added bass part (cf. nos. 20, 21, and 28). This is due, in part, to the fact that the soprano

---

[1] The B section begins at the editorial double bar in m. 13.

[2] In his edition of the complete works of Dufay, Heinrich Besseler includes this chanson among the works of doubtful authorship. Of the ten sources containing this piece, one ascribes it to Dufay, one to Binchois, and the remaining eight give no composer.

and tenor lie unusually close together—so much so that in measures 13–15 the soprano actually drops below the tenor.

Like all the chansons of the fifteenth century, this piece was intended for solo performance, and is beautifully suited for countertenor and tenor.[3] The only instruments possible for the contratenor part are the bass viol or lute; they may also double. One may well wish to make a few changes of scoring within the piece, particularly in view of the recurring A sections. (Changes of scoring are completely in accord with the nature of pieces that derive their form from repetition.) However, under no condition should the performance become a patchwork of different sounds. Rather, one should decide upon one basic scoring for the opening section and *some* of the others, so that the piece has an overall unity of sound. Some of the other sections may have contrasting scorings. Further unity can be achieved by using one of the contrasting scorings more than once. Beginning, then, with the basic scoring of countertenor, tenor, and bass viol or lute or both, the following alternatives or additions are suggested: (1) that the tenor part not be sung, but instead played by tenor or bass viol, vielle, lute, or portative organ; (2) that the top voice be doubled by Renaissance descant flute, portative organ, or alto recorder (all an octave higher), or Renaissance bass flute or portative organ in unison; (3) that the tenor voice be doubled by tenor or bass viol (only if the top voice is also being doubled at this point); (4) that the top voice be sung and the two lower parts be played by lute; (5) that all parts be played with the top voice performed by vielle, treble or tenor viol, or tenor recorder if the piece has been transposed up a minor third (see below).

This chanson may, of course, be sung by a solo alto. Transposition a minor third higher makes performance possible by soprano and countertenor. Any of the above scorings will work, with the one change that soprano recorder replaces alto recorder—though such high octave doubling may prove too bright for this piece. A much better alternative in this case is to double the soprano voice in unison with tenor recorder.

Helpful as the above discussion may prove to be, it will be of little use to the performer unless the performance is infused with the lovely, warm tenderness of the text. Phrases must be gently but clearly shaped, with great sensitivity to the many melodic and rhythmic nuances within them. Good solo singers, who bring a sensitive, flexible, and searching approach to their art, will find this chanson—and many others of this period—truly rewarding.

SOURCE: Trent, Castello del Buon Consiglio, Ms. 90, fol. 352′.
MODERN EDITION: *Dufay, *Zwölf geistliche und weltliche Werke,* ed. H. Besseler, Das Chorwerk, no. 19, Wolfenbüttel, 1932, p. 24; Dufay, *Opera omnia,* ed. H. Besseler, VI, Rome, 1962, p. 109.
TEXT:

1. Je ne vis onques la pareille
   De vous, ma gracieuse dame.

2. Vostre beauté m'est, sur mon ame,
   sur toutes aultres non pareille

3. En vous voiant je m'esmerveille
   Et dis qu'est ceci nostre dame?

1. Je ne vis . . .

4. Vostre tres grant doulceur resveille
   Mon esprit, et mon oeil entame

5. Mon cuer, dont dire puissans blame,
   Puisqu'a vous servir m'apareille.

1. Je ne vis . . .

2. Vostre beauté . . .

---

[3] A vivid account of a most colorful contemporary performance of this chanson is quoted at length by Gustave Reese in *Music in the Renaissance,* rev. ed., New York, 1959, pp. 57 f.

TRANSLATION:

1. Never have I seen your like,
   Gracious lady.

2. Your beauty, upon my soul,
   To me is beyond compare.

3. Seeing you I marvel and ask myself:
   Who is this lady of ours?

1. Never have . . .

4. Your great sweetness awakens
   My mind, and my eye penetrates

5. My heart—which is great blame—
   Thus compelling me to serve you.

1. Never have . . .

2. Your beauty . . .

PERFORMANCE SUGGESTIONS: ♩ = c. 82; also, see above.

MODERN SCORING: flute in place of Renaissance flute or recorders, viola in place of vielle or tenor viol, cello in place of bass viol, guitar in place of lute.

Je ne vis oncques la pareille

20 ∽

HAYNE VAN GHIZEGHEM (b. c. 1445)

Alles regretz

The entire brief life of Hayne van Ghizeghem was spent in the service of the Burgundian court. His name first appears in court records as a boy apprentice in 1457; later he was appointed singer in the royal chapel and became personal valet to both Philip the Good and his successor Charles the Bold. He accompanied Charles at the disastrous seige of Beauvais in 1472 and probably fell in that battle since there is no mention of him after that date.

The musical output of his short life is correspondingly small. All his works are chansons, all rondeaux *a 3* in duple meter. Among them are some of the most famous songs of the early sixteenth century; *Alles regretz,* one of the most celebrated, comes down to us in no less than twenty-three sources. Its tenor part became a favorite *cantus firmus,* and was used in Masses by Josquin and Compère as well as in later chanson settings by Compère, Agricola, and Senfl. Its popularity continued well into the sixteenth century, for it was one of the few Burgundian pieces copied into the late Tudor "Henry VIII Ms.," which is the source for our edition. Although Hayne may have written the texts for most of his chansons, that of *Alles regretz* is by Jean II, duke of Bourbon and cousin and brother-in-law of Charles the Bold.[1]

Regrets, a favorite theme of fifteenth-century poetry, provided the subject for many chansons of the time. (In addition to *Alles regretz,* these include *Tous les regretz, Venez regrets, Mille regretz, Trop de regretz,* and *Plusiers regretz.*)

Fashionable though this melancholy was, it seems likely that some later *regrets* chansons may have been composed in sympathetic tribute to Marguerite of Austria. That highly cultivated and capable princess, duchess of Savoy and, later, regent of the Netherlands, presided over one of the most brilliant artistic centers in Europe at Malines. Like her renowned Italian contemporary Isabelle d'Este, Marguerite attracted many of the greatest musicians, artists, writers, and humanists to her court. Twice widowed at an early age and later bitterly grieved at the untimely death in 1506 of her brother Philip, king of Castile, she wore mourning to the end of her life. In her own eyes, Marguerite was a tragic victim of fate; her wryly despairing motto was "Fortune infortune fort une" (fortune makes one very unfortunate).[2]

Like the preceding piece by Dufay, *Alles regretz* is a rondeau; its apparent AB form is expanded by the poetic form into ABAAABAB. In our edition, only the first two lines of text are given with the music; the complete text is given below. (See the commentary for the preceding piece for an explanation of the complete rondeau form.)

Though Hayne's birthdate around 1445 makes him a contemporary of Josquin, he is stylistically a Burgundian. His chansons retain some features of those by Dufay and Ockeghem—especially their long, intricate lines and their lack of imitation.

---

[1] Since the text is lacking in our source, we have adapted it from Helen Hewitt's edition of the *Odhecaton.*

[2] Much of the preceding information about Marguerite is taken from Martin Picker's article "The Chanson Albums of Marguerite of Austria," *Annales musicologiques,* VI (1964), pp. 145 ff. See also Martin Picker, *The Chanson Albums of Marguerite of Austria,* Berkeley, 1965.

Different from the older masters, though, is Hayne's contratenor part, for it has now achieved full status. No longer content with crisscrossing the tenor part and generally filling in, it lies consistently below the tenor, providing a true bass line with as much melodic richness as the upper parts. This feature, plus the lack of "under-third" cadences and the relatively equal sharing of melodic activity among all three voice parts, foreshadows the emerging Netherlands style.

Performance of *Alles regretz* calls for solo voice, with tenor viol on the highest part and bass viol on the contratenor. The written pitch is suitable for high baritone, but, because of the high F in measure 44, transposition a tone lower might be better. Transposition a tone higher will bring the vocal part into good tenor range. The vocal sound should be warm but not heavy. As with the many Burgundian chansons of sad or melancholy character, the performance of this song must be intense but never doleful. Rather, a mixture of tenderness and grace best describes the quality of performance to be aimed for. The performers must make unusually long phrases hold together, and the many lovely rises and falls within the phrases must be sensitively followed with subtle dynamic shadings.

SOURCE: *British Museum Add. Ms. 31922, fols. 2'–3.

MODERN EDITION: *Harmonice musices Odhecaton A,* ed. H. Hewitt, Cambridge, Mass., 1942, pp. 341 f.

TEXT:

1. Alles regretz vuidiez de ma présence,
   Alles allieurs quérir vostre acointance,
   Asses aves tourmenté mon las coeur.

2. Rempli de deuil pour estre serviteur
   D'une sans per que j'ay aymée d'enfance.

3. Fait luy aves longuement ceste offence.
   Ou est celuy qui point soit né en France
   Qui endurast ce mortel deshonneur?

1. Alles regretz . . .

4. N'y tournes plus, car, par ma conscience,
   Se plus vous voy prochain de ma plasance,
   Devant chascun vous feray tel honneur

5. Que l'on dira que la main d'ung seigneur
   Vous a bien mys à la male meschance.

1. Alles regretz . . .

TRANSLATION:

1. Go, regrets, out of my presence,
   Seek your company elsewhere;
   Enough have you tormented my weary heart

2. Filled with sorrow from being the servant
   Of her, beyond compare, whom I have loved
   Since childhood.

3. Long have you offended my heart this way.
   Where is there anyone born throughout the realm of France
   Who would endure this deadly dishonor?

1. Go, regrets . . .
4. Turn hither no more, for, upon my wits,
   Should I see you near again,
   Before all will I do you such a turn

5. That they will say that the hand of a mighty lord
   Has brought you such misfortune.

1. Go, regrets . . .

PERFORMANCE SUGGESTIONS: ♩ = c. 74; also, see above.

Alles regretz

S.

Moderately fast

T.

Al - les re - gretz

Ct.

vui - diez de ma_____ pré - sen -

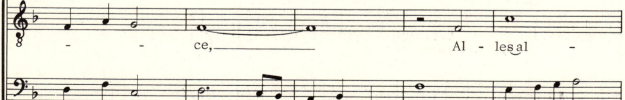

- ce,_____ Al - les al -

Rem - pli de deuil_____ pour es - tre

ser - vi - teur D'u - ne

sans per_____ que j'ay ay - mé - -

e d'en - fan - - - ce.

*d'' in original.

21 ❧

ANTOINE BUSNOIS (d. 1492)

Je ne puis vivre ainsi tousjours

Antoine de Busne, known as Busnois, was apparently a pupil of Ockeghem, and had a brilliant career at the Burgundian court from 1467, under Charles the Bold, to the death of Mary of Burgundy in 1482. He was a poet as well, and many of his chansons (including the one presented here) were settings of his own texts. He was also a priest and held several church posts, including that of *rector cantoriae* at St. Sauveur at Bruges until his death in 1492.

Though various sacred works of Busnois survive, his chansons are his most outstanding pieces. Their great popularity in his own time is shown by their appearance in many contemporary collections. Of the seventy-odd chansons, only two are in Italian, one being the famous *Fortuna desperata* (no. 29), on which Obrecht (see no. 3) and Josquin based Masses. His chansons, with their lovely melodic lines, supple rhythmic nuances, more "modern" harmony, and masterly use of imitation, show his remarkable range of skill and imagination.

Occasional examples of the technique of imitation can be found in isolated pieces as far back as the thirteenth century, and imitation is the very essence of the Italian *caccia* and French *chace*—those canonic extravaganzas of the fourteenth century. But extensive imitation does not occur with any real frequency until the works of Busnois.[1] In his music, it becomes a favorite technique, and we may regard him as preparing

the way for its widespread use. Imitative technique, the single most characteristic feature of later Renaissance music, was to have a profound and far-reaching effect on the development of Western music for the next two hundred fifty years.

Je ne puis vivre, in ABBAA form, is a *bergerette*—a popular late fifteenth-century form that is itself a shorter version of the much older *virelai,* one of the medieval *formes fixes.* This beautiful song is a fine example of Busnois's gift for exquisite melodic lines. The two treble parts, highly imitative and at times even in canon, unfold in lovely, arching contours. Their expressiveness is due also to the constantly varied rhythms, the asymmetrical arrangement of long and short notes, the many gentle and expressive offbeats, and the irregular phrase lengths. The contratenor, though playing a somewhat supportive role, shares these same virtues. One is especially struck by the rising canonic sequence in measure 13–19, with its effect of accelerated movement and shifting tonicizations. The change from triple to duple meter for the second section plus this section's homophonic opening are typical of *bergerettes* of this period. An interesting detail is that Busnois has included in the text the name of his beloved mistress, Jacqueline d'Hacqueville, as an acrostic: the first letter of each line of the poem spells out JAQUELJNEDAQVEVJL. Her name appears, by various other methods, in three other of his chansons.

Performance is for solo voice and two instrumental parts. The written pitch is ideal for alto; it may be transposed a tone higher for soprano,

---

[1] Imitation does not refer here primarily to canonic writing that involves an extended melodic line, but to the repetition, at the unison, fifth, or octave, of a short melodic motive in close succession in other voice parts.

a tone lower for countertenor, or a fifth lower for tenor. For the untexted treble part, treble viol or vielle can best match the dynamic shadings of the solo voice, though tenor recorder can also be used if the piece is transposed a tone higher. Bass viol, lute, or both are the most suitable instruments for the contratenor part. This song could be performed by two equal voices, with the addition of text to the second part.

SOURCE: Dijon Ms. 517, fol. 34.

MODERN EDITION: *Trois chansoniers français du XVe siècle, eds. E. Droz, G. Thibault, and Y. Rokseth (Paris, 1927), pp. 63 ff.

TRANSLATION:

1. No longer can I live this way
   Unless I have some comfort—
   An hour at least and more
   In my suffering.
   Then forevermore shall I serve love faithfully—
   Until death.

2. Lady, noble of name and arms,
   Answer this plea.

3. My eyes are hot with tears,
   That you might take pity on me.

4. As for me, I die straight away—
   Wakeful at night, tossing a hundred times,
   Loudly crying vengeance to God, for wrongly
   Do I drown in tears
   While help fails me in my need
   And pity sleeps.

PERFORMANCE SUGGESTIONS: ♩ = c. 76; also, see above.

MODERN SCORING:

A. flute
Ct. guitar

Je ne puis vivre ainsi tousjours

---

[2] If the indicated proportional tempo relationship between this section and the preceding one is observed, the $\frac{2}{4}$ section may be too slow. The editor's suggestion is to take this section ♩ = ♩ (see the Introduction, pp. 2–3).

22

JOSQUIN DES PREZ (c. 1445–1521)

Petite camusette

In secular as in sacred music, Josquin's genius has created works that are examples *par excellence* of their genre. His more than fifty chansons show an extraordinary range of structure, polyphonic richness, and breadth of expression. The old *formes fixes* (see the three preceding pieces) have by and large been discarded in favor of the more modern symmetry of a whole range of ABA and strophic forms, many of them using his favorite device, the canon.

Petite camusette, in ABA form, is typical of Josquin's inventiveness. Unlike the Burgundian chansons, which are conceived as one sung part with instruments, this song is written in the richly polyphonic texture of Josquin's motets, with all voice parts equally important. *Petite camusette* is a popular song that has the tonal clarity and simple, strongly shaped phrases typical of many popular tunes of the day. (There are numerous other settings of this tune, including one by Ockeghem and two later ones by Willaert.) In Josquin's setting, the tune appears in canon in the middle voices, a treatment that adds greatly to the polyphonic liveliness of the piece. The strettolike opening has a wonderful effect, with the voices entering one measure apart, each heralding the coming tune by stating its first few notes, and with the complete tune entering last in the two middle voices. Once the canon has entered, the two upper voices pair off in a lively dialogue of their own, taking turns with several short motives. The two lower parts similarly pair off with their own collection of short motives, and spend most of the time imitating each other. The

six-part texture consists, therefore, of three distinct pairs of voices—high, middle, and low—each pair with its own melodic material distinct from the others. This pairing arrangement is emphasized by the fact that the two voices of each pair lie in exactly the same pitch range. The ever-changing combination of parts gives an almost kaleidoscopic effect to the polyphonic texture; and because there are often only four or five parts present, the six-part writing becomes unusually transparent.

This piece readily lends itself to a wide variety of scorings, several of which are given below. Of course, it can be performed well with voices only —preferably one on a part—at the written pitch (or a tone or a minor third higher) by two sopranos, two tenors, and two baritones. Viols could double the two tenors in order to set off the canon from the other parts by their contrasting timbre. (Instrumental doubling on the other parts is not recommended since it would destroy some of the lightness of these parts.) Perhaps the most winning performance results when only the canonic parts are sung while the other parts are played. This has two advantages: not only does the sung canon stand out clearly from the instrumental timbre of the other parts, but the light, agile character of the outer parts is probably rendered most effectively by instruments. Also very effective is an entirely instrumental performance, provided the canonic parts are slightly more prominent than the others and have a contrasting timbre. A twofold performance of this delightful piece would be most welcome.

SOURCE: *Le septiesme livre contenant vingt et quatre chansons,* T. Susato, Antwerp, 1545.

MODERN EDITION: *Josquin des Prez, Werken,* ed. A. Smijers, *Wereldlijke Werken,* I, Amsterdam, 1924, pp. 43 f.

TRANSLATION:

Pretty little snub nose, you'll be the death of me. Robin and Marion go off to the fair woods. They go arm in arm; they have fallen asleep. Pretty little snub nose, you'll be the death of me.

PERFORMANCE SUGGESTIONS: ♩ = c. 108

I—At written pitch, or a tone or a minor third higher:

S. and Q.	two sopranos (or mezzo-sopranos)
Ct. and T.	two tenors (perhaps doubled by two viols, any size)
Se. and B.	two baritones
or	
S. and Q.	two tenor recorders or treble viols
Ct. and T.	two tenors
Se. and B.	bass viols or lutes
or	
S. and Q.	two treble viols
Ct. and T.	two alto shawms
Se. and B.	two bass viols
or	
S. and Q.	two tenor recorders or treble viols
Ct. and T.	two alto krummhorns
Se. and B.	two bass viols or lutes
or	
S. and Q.	two tenor recorders
Ct. and T.	two tenor or bass viols
Se. and B.	two lutes

II—A fifth higher:

S. and Q.	two treble viols
Ct. and T.	two soprano shawms (*mp–mf*)
Se. and B.	two bass or tenor viols
or	
S. and Q.	two alto recorders or treble viols
Ct. and T.	two soprano krummhorns
Se. and B.	two bass or tenor viols, or lutes
or	
S. and Q.	two alto recorders
Ct. and T.	two tenor or bass viols
Se. and B.	two lutes

III—An octave higher:

S. and Q.	two soprano recorders
Ct. and T.	two soprano shawms (*mp–mf*)
Se. and B.	two tenor or treble viols
or	
S. and Q.	two soprano recorders
Ct. and T.	two soprano krummhorns
Se. and B.	two tenor or treble viols, or lutes
or	
S. and Q.	two soprano recorders
Ct. and T.	two treble viols
Se. and B.	two lutes

MODERN SCORING: substitute flute for recorder, oboe or English horn for shawm or krummhorn, bassoon or cello for tenor or bass viol, violin for treble viol, and guitar for lute.

Petite camusette

23 〜

HEINRICH ISAAC (c. 1450–1517)

Innsbruck, ich muss dich lassen

Near the end of the fifteenth century, at the court of the great patron Maximilian, a new German musical style was taking shape. This new music combined the richly imitative, free-flowing polyphony of the Netherlands with the clearly shaped and strongly tonal melodic style of the native German tradition. Isaac, that astonishingly versatile Netherlander, cannot be given sole credit for this synthesis, yet it was he more than any other single composer who brought it about. In the process, he set German music on the course that was to lead to the momentous developments of later centuries.

Though Isaac's last years were spent in his beloved Florence, he had earlier lived in Vienna and Innsbruck as resident composer to Maximilian's court. *Innsbruck, ich muss dich lassen* (Innsbruck, I must leave you) (23b), today probably the most famous song of the entire early Renaissance, was undoubtedly composed as a fond farewell to the court and to the town he knew and loved. The significance of this piece extends far beyond its immediate period, however; in three basic ways it foreshadows much of the later development of the Lutheran chorale: the melody is given to the top voice, not to the tenor (as was usual in the lieder of Isaac's time); the writing is predominantly homophonic; and the short silences between phrases give the piece a sectional rather than a continuous character. This very tune, newly fitted with a sacred text based on the original secular one, actually reappeared later as the chorale *O Welt ich muss dich lassen*

(O world, I must leave thee), subsequently used both by Bach and by Brahms.[1]

Though at first glance one of the simplest pieces of music ever written, the totally asymmetrical structure of this tiny masterpiece is highly sophisticated. This asymmetry stems from the differing lengths of the various phrases as well as from the metrical irregularities within most of them. (Of course, the bar lines here have absolutely no meaning in the modern sense.) In contrast to the first two phrases, the very short third phrase moves entirely in quarter notes. The last phrase and its repeat are extended on the word "Elend" (misery) by the little groups of eighth notes, emphasized by the alto doubling in parallel fourths and echoed by the tenor one beat later. These irregularities of design stand out all the more, clothed as they are in the simple fabric of homophony. Finally, one must mention the lovely effect of the triad on the lowered seventh in the fifth and thirteenth measures[2] and the modal treatment of the supertonic in the third phrase.

Nothing could be more different from this setting than Isaac's earlier one (23a). Here, it is his

---

[1] Among Bach's chorales, the melody may be found with the still later title *Nun ruhen alle Wälder*.

[2] Such "lowered-seventh triads"—to use the terminology of the common practice period—are by no means rare in early Renaissance music (cf. no. 29). It is self-evident that their occurrence invariably avoids a tritone; yet it seems unreasonable to deny the possibility that composers in the fifteenth century were already well aware of the harmonic aspects of music, and that such things as the E-flat harmonies in *Innsbruck* were deliberately planned.

Netherlands style that is predominant. The canonic treatment of the tune in the two middle voices completely bridges over the phrase endings of the melody, giving it the long, continuous line favored in the Flemish style. The top part and the bass, whose longer phrases are completely independent of each other as well as of the canon, further contribute to the free-flowing quality of this setting.

Because of the absence of text, one might assume that Isaac intended this earlier setting for instruments. But the fact that he used the identical piece as the Christe II in his *Missa Carminum* makes it perfectly clear that it was, to him, just as appropriate for vocal performance. Therefore, all four parts can certainly be given text, and in that case, the piece can be sung by tenor, tenor, tenor, bass. Perhaps better, the canonic inner voices can be sung (tenor, tenor) while the two outer parts are played, which will clearly distinguish the canon from the outer parts.[3] Because of the gentle expressiveness of the piece, treble (or tenor) and bass viols are the most suitable instruments. Of course, this setting can be performed purely instrumentally, with viols on all four parts.

The later, simpler version of *Innsbruck* (23b) is perhaps most effectively performed by voices alone (countertenor or alto, tenor, baritone, bass), although a good performance can be achieved with viols doubling the voices. This setting can also be scored for solo countertenor or alto, and three viols. S.A.T.B. performance will also be successful if the pitch is raised between a whole step and a fourth. Since this song is so short, it should certainly be performed more than once through. For this reason, the texts of the second and third verses are given below. An especially pleasing performance results if both settings are combined into a large two- or three-part form, going without pause from one setting to the other. If one setting is used for all three verses, contrasting scorings should be used.

SOURCES: (*23a*) Basel, Universitäts Bibliothek F. X. fols. 22, 23, 24 (tenor missing); Munich, Bibliothek des Universitäts Mss., fols. 328–331 (soprano missing). (*23b*) G. Forster, *Ein ausszug guter alter und newer teutscher Liedlein zu singen und auff allerley Instrumenten zu gebrauchen, sonderlich ausserlesen,* J. Petreio, Nuremberg, 1539.

MODERN EDITION: *Denkmäler der Tonkunst in Österreich, Jahrg. XIV, Teil I, Band 28, pp. 15, 83.

TEXT OF VERSES 2 AND 3:
Gross Leid muss ich jetzt tragen,
das ich allein tu klagen
dem liebsten Buhlen mein.
Ach Lieb, nun lass mich Armen
im Herzen dein erbarmen,
dass ich muss dannen sein.

Mein Trost ob allen Weiben,
dein tu ich ewig bleiben,
stet treu, der Ehren fromm.
Nun muss dich Gott bewahren,
in aller Tugend sparen,
bis dass ich wiederkomm.

TRANSLATION:
Innsbruck, I must leave you
I am going on my way
into a foreign land.
My joy is taken from me,
I know not how to regain it,
while in such misery.

I must now endure great pain
which I confide only
to my dearest love.

---

[3] The editors have supplied text for the two canonic parts.

O beloved, find pity in your heart
for me,
that I must part from you.

My comfort above all other women,
I shall always be yours,
forever faithful in honor true.
May the good Lord protect you
and keep you in your virtue
for me, till I return.

PERFORMANCE SUGGESTIONS: 23a: ♩ = c. 60; 23b: ♩ = c. 54
NUMBER OF VOICES: four solo voices, or choral ensemble of twelve to thirty-two voices.

The following are several suggested plans for a three-way performance (as discussed above) using both versions of the song.

first verse	*second verse*	*third verse*
later version (*23b*)	earlier version (*23a*)	later version (*23b*)
voices only	two solo voices and	any scoring given for the first verse
or	two viols	
voices doubled by viols	*or*	
or	four viols	
solo voice and three viols	*or*	
or	voices only	
four viols		

MODERN SCORING: violin, two violas, cello.

a. Gross Leid muss ich jetzt tragen

(*182*)   Heinrich Isaac

liebsten buhlen mein. Ach Lieb, nun lass mich Ar-

mein. Ach Lieb, nun lass mich Ar-men im

men im Her-zen dein er-bar-

Her-zen dein er-bar-men, dass

men, dass ich muss dan - - - - nen sein.

ich muss dan - - - - nen sein.

b. *Innsbruck, ich muss dich lassen*

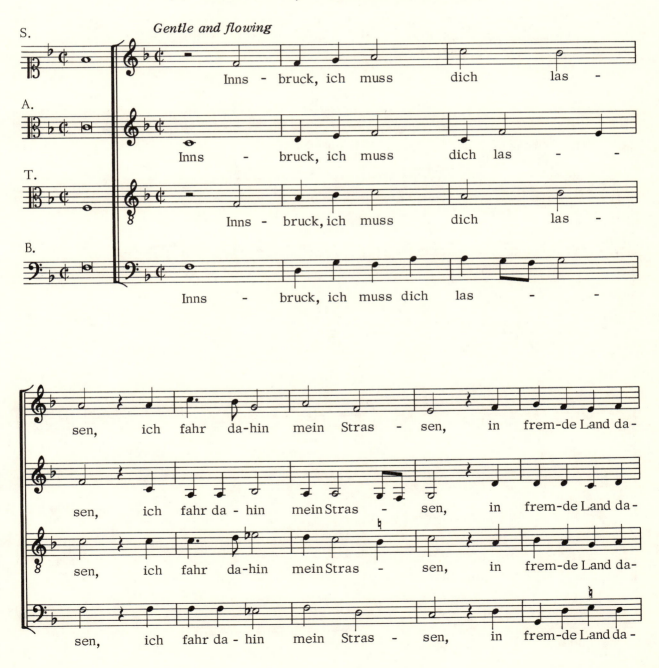

24 &

MICHELE PESENTI (fl. 1500)

Dal lecto me levava

Although Italy had produced outstanding music during the later Middle Ages and would see another brilliant flowering in the madrigal of the sixteenth century, the fifteenth century did not produce a single native composer of any consequence. There was no lack of musical activity, however, as the various courts vied with each other in splendor and artistic excellence. But this brilliant musical activity was due solely to that dazzling array of first-rate Flemish composers who, born and trained in the north, came for long periods of employ to the Italian courts. In the first collections of printed music published in Venice by Ottaviano dei Petrucci (c. 1500), not one Italian composer appears; all are northerners. Scarcely one Italian name can be found in the records of the papal choir. Even the music tutors in the aristocratic households were foreigners!

During this time there was virtually no musical or literary contact between the wealthy aristocracy, educated in Latin and Greek as well as the arts, and the common citizenry, schooled in none of these. But the common people had their own arts, including a vast quantity of popular poetry, much of which they recited to improvised music. Toward the end of the fifteenth century, the courtly and popular forms of music and literature began to interact.

Isabella d'Este, one of the most cultivated women of the entire Renaissance, made her court at Mantua one of the most brilliant artistic centers in Italy and did much to establish Italian as a language worthy of serious music. She enjoyed poetry to its fullest only when it was sung, and employed one of the leading poets of the time (and a skilled singer), Serafino dall' Aquila. Also at her court were two of the best new native composers, Bartolomeo Tromboncino (see no. 16) and Marco Cara. From these talented Italians, under the fond, encouraging gaze of Isabella, was born a new national style of secular music, embodied in short songs collectively known as *frottole*. (A national secular musical style was similarly emerging at this time in Spain; see no. 26.)

These winning pieces, half aristocratic and half popular, were soon cultivated in other courts in northern Italy. The songs featured a simple melodic line in the top voice set over a predominantly chordal texture, and moved in short, clear-cut phrases. The natural stresses of the poetry were faithfully maintained, resulting in simple, clear, and often dancelike rhythms. The harmonic style, rooted firmly in the simplest progressions using especially the tonic and dominant chords, brought to this music a hitherto nonexistent tonal clarity. The melodious directness of this new Italian style, in its turn, strongly influenced the next generation of northern composers and laid the foundation for the development of the madrigal.

Very little is known of Michele Pesenti's life, other than that he was born in Verona and became a priest. Thirty-three of his *frottole* were included in Petrucci's printed collections. His delightful *Dal lecto me levava* shows a charming blend of lightweight verse and elegant counterpoint. Its neat structure, pointed declamation, and equally conceived parts show the way to the forthcoming French chanson and madrigal. Its naturalistic bird imitations (set to the word "gru") are a sparkling reminder of Josquin's famous cricket song *El Grillo*. "La gru" is the Italian for crane as well as the nickname of the courtesan who is the master's early visitor.

This song may be performed by four solo voices or small choral ensemble, either with or without instruments. Depending on the complement of singers, transposition may be necessary. The two inner parts, having the same range and *tessitura*, must be sung by similar voices. The piece is also very effective performed instrumentally. Several scorings are suggested below. Because this song is very short, it is best to give a twofold or threefold performance. A very good plan is to perform it first with instruments only; second, with voices only; and third, with voices and instruments combined. Regardless of scoring, the performance must have a sparkling, lighthearted, fun-loving atmosphere.

SOURCE: *Frottole, Libro Primo*, Petrucci, Venice, 1504.

MODERN EDITION: *Karnevalslieder der Renaissance*, ed. K. Westphal, Das Chorwerk, no. 43, Wolfenbüttel, 1936, pp. 7 ff.

TRANSLATION:

I was rising from bed to serve the Signor; just then his servant, La Grua, arrived (*gru, gru gru*). The sweet "ambassador" said, "Don't get up, go back to sleep" . . . (*gru, gru, gru*). Would that everyone said (*gru, gru, gru*), "Go back to sleep."

PERFORMANCE SUGGESTIONS: ♩ = c. 104.

NUMBER OF VOICES: four solo voices, preferably *a cappella;* or small vocal ensemble (twelve to twenty voices).

S.	altos or mezzo-sopranos	with soprano krummhorn or treble viol; and/or soprano recorder
A.	tenors (and altos)	with also krummhorn or tenor viol, and/or tenor recorder
T.	tenors (and altos)	with alto krummhorn or tenor viol, and/or tenor recorder
B.	baritones/basses	with tenor krummhorn,[1] bass viol, or regal

Lute may be added to any of the above scorings, playing either one or two voice parts or a short score; or it can be used in place of other instruments if solo voices are used or if the choral ensemble is very light. Krummhorns and viols may be mixed in any combination.

INSTRUMENTAL PERFORMANCE:

S. soprano krummhorn or treble viol
A. alto krummhorn or tenor viol
T. alto krummhorn or tenor viol
B. tenor krummhorn,[1] bass viol, or regal
    or
S. soprano or alto recorder
A. treble viol
T. treble viol
B. soprano krummhorn [2]
    or
S. soprano or alto recorder
A. tenor recorder
T. tenor recorder
B. bass recorder

MODERN SCORING: Substitute flute for recorders, viola for treble and tenor viols, cello for bass viol, oboe for soprano krummhorn, English horn for alto krummhorn, bassoon for tenor krummhorn or regal.

---

[1] Possible only if the piece is transposed a tone higher.
[2] See n. 1 above.

Dal lecto me levava

25 &

ANONYMOUS (c. 1500)

Mia benigna fortuna

Among the most brilliant musicians at the northern Italian courts around 1500 were virtuoso performers on the lute, viols, and keyboard instruments. They played their own original compositions in free, improvisatory style, along with their instrumental arrangements of already existing vocal music. Much evidence points to the fact that the lute was the most favored instrument and that lute and solo voice were a favorite combination. Baldassare Castiglione, in his *Il cortegiano* (1528), gives a clear image of the well-rounded courtier of the time as well as a vivid account of contemporary society. He indicates that he especially likes performance by solo voice and lute. Both Bartolomeo Tromboncino and Marco Cara were famous for their singing to the lute, further attesting to the popularity of this type of performance. There was an increasing number of amateur performers, some undoubtedly quite gifted, who must have greatly admired the virtuosi and who wanted to emulate them. Petrucci, quick to see in this growing number of amateurs a whole new market rapidly developing for printed collections of solo lute music and lute songs, published six collections for this clientele between 1507 and 1511. The first three books contain music for lute alone: arrangements of already existing vocal music, *ricercare* freely composed in an improvisatory style well suited to the idiom of the lute, and dances (see no. 33). The last two volumes contain mainly songs arranged for solo voice and lute, almost all *frottole* from the large number that had already appeared in Petrucci's earlier publications.

It was a simple matter to adapt these homophonic four-voice pieces. The highest part was given to the solo voice, while the tenor and bass parts were merely written out in lute tablature and the alto part omitted. Though omitting a part may strike us today as an inexcusable crudity, the two-part accompaniment sounds quite well on the lute. Petrucci was not the only publisher to make such adaptations. In 1529 Pierre Attaingnant published some three-part arrangements of four-part chansons, and earlier, Arnolt Schlick omitted the alto part in a dozen lute-song intabulations printed in 1512. Such simplification of accompaniments clearly brought these pieces within reach of the increasing number of amateur lute players. The large repertoire of already existing four-part music provided plenty of material for immediate publication, taking the fullest advantage of the new trend and, at the same time, fostering it.

The anonymous *Mia benigna fortuna* first appeared as a four-part piece in Petrucci's ninth book of *frottole*, published in 1508. The version given here comes from his first lute-song collection of 1509 entitled *Tenor and Bass in Tablature with the Soprano in Pitch Notation, to Sing and Play with the Lute, Book One*. It is a setting of the first stanza from Petrarch's sestina on the death of his beloved Laura—verses that later inspired such madrigal composers as Arcadelt, Rore, Lassus, Monte, Wert, and Marenzio. Petrarch's moving words are set in a simple, syllabic style. The few poignant upward leaps and the prevailing descending stepwise motion, beautifully express the melancholy and despair of the text.

At written pitch, this song is ideal for solo countertenor; for tenor, transpose down a minor third, and for soprano, up a major third or (for a light soprano) an augmented fourth. If a lutenist is not available, guitar or harpsichord may be used. Lacking any plucked instrument, treble (or tenor) and bass viols may be used with complete success. To extend the song, it may be performed twice, or even three times,[1] once as an instrumental piece. In that case, treble viol or vielle is the most suitable instrument for the gentle, expressive character of the top line. This hauntingly beautiful song must be performed with tenderness and sensitive phrasing by both singer and instrumentalist.

SOURCE: *F. Bossinensis, *Tenori e contrabassi intabulati . . . Lib. I,* Petrucci, Venice, 1509, fol. 23.

TRANSLATION:
> My kind fortune and happy life,
> The clear days and tranquil nights,
> And the gentle sighs and "sweet style"
> Accustomed to resound in verse and rhyme;
> You turn suddenly to pain and tears
> Which make me hate life and long for death.

PERFORMANCE SUGGESTIONS: ♩ = c. 54; also, see above.

---

[1] The original four-part version of this *frottola* has five verses.

Mia benigna fortuna

Mia be - ni - gna for - tu - na e'l vi - ver lie - to, i chia - ri gior - n'e le tran - quil - le not - ti,

ei so - a - vi sos - pir' e'l dol - ce sti - le, che

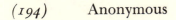

so - le - a ri - so - na - r'in   ver - s'e'n   ri - me,

Vol - ti su - bi - ta - men - t'in do - glia e pian - to

O - diar me fan - no vi - ta e___ bra - mar mor - te.

26

JUAN DEL ENCINA (c. 1468–1529)

Triste España sin ventura

As far back as the thirteenth century, Spain, like much of Europe, was influenced mainly by French music. France maintained her musical supremacy until the end of the fifteenth century, when Italy, herself richly nurtured by the new music from France, emerged as a major musical influence in Europe. But toward the end of the century, Spanish composers began to break away from these foreign influences. Absorbing some of the traits of native Castilian folk music, they produced a large quantity of short, secular art songs that were uniquely Spanish in flavor. This flowering of a new national style [1] was due in part to the far more stable conditions in Spain following the union of Castile and Aragon in 1474 under the Catholic Monarchs Ferdinand and Isabella. Queen Isabella was an avid music lover, and employed a great many singers and instrumentalists at the court and the royal chapel.

The large repertoire of secular songs that appeared during this Golden Age soon found its way into extensive collections called *cancioneros,* the counterpart of the French *chansonniers.* Of the many that have survived, the most important is the *Cancionero musical de Palacio,* containing over four hundred fifty songs. These pieces, in their essential features, are first cousins of the Italian *frottole* (see nos. 24 and 25). They are short works, *a 3* or *a 4,* mostly in chordal style, and clearly tonal, using mainly the principal harmonies of the key. The main melody is in the top voice, and moves in clearly articulated phrases. These simple but winning tunes—often

pungent and catchy, but sometimes austere—betray their unmistakable folk origin, and seem to mirror those flashes of gaiety set against the somber backdrop of fanatic religious fervor that characterized Spanish life. The composer most generously represented in the *Cancionero musical de Palacio* is Juan del Encina.

Born near Salamanca around 1468, Juan del Encina received at least part of his musical training as a singer at Salamanca Cathedral. He rose rapidly in the courtly world, becoming master of ceremonies at the palace of the duke of Alba. A dramatist as well as a composer, he put both talents to good use in the production of numerous eclogues—pastoral plays that included music—which were popular in Spain in the sixteenth century and were frequently performed at the duke's palace. Encina's eclogues made an important contribution to the early development of the Spanish theater. Later in his career he was appointed prior of León, where he remained until his death around 1529. His compositions are exclusively secular, almost all composed before he was twenty-five, during his years as a courtier.

Triste España sin ventura is a fine example of Encina's style. The fact that it was written on the death of Isabella surely accounts for its more-than-usual mixture of sadness, tenderness, and austerity. Its utter simplicity belies its art. The four phrases, uneven in length, are subtly different in contour and rhythmic shape. The tonal ambiguity of the first three cadences is only clarified retrospectively with the final appearance of the real tonic, G minor.

Solo voice with lute (or viols), four solo voices,

---

[1] For comments on the similar emergence of a native secular style in Italy, see no. 24.

or small vocal ensemble are all equally successful performance possibilities. Since the voice parts lie in normal relation to one another and all have a very narrow compass, virtually any complement of vocal ranges can be perfectly accommodated by transposition in either direction. This tiny masterpiece begs to be heard more than once. In a twofold performance, the most logical plan is to have solo voice first, followed by four sung parts. In a threefold performance, an instrumental version—lute solo (playing all four parts, with the top voice elaborated), or treble viol or vielle with lute accompaniment—can be placed either at the beginning, or between solo-voice and vocal-ensemble versions. A sparing use of expressive ornamentation on the top line can be very effective.

SOURCE: Madrid, Biblioteca del Palacio Real, *Cancionero musical de Palacio*, fols. 55′–56.

MODERN EDITION: *La Música en la Corte de los Reyes Católicos: Polifonia profana—Cancionero musical de Palacio*, ed. H. Anglès, Barcelona, 1947, p. 109.

TRANSLATION:
Sad Spain, without a future,
All should weep for you;
Forsaken by joy,
Which is never to return to you!

PERFORMANCE SUGGESTIONS: ♩ = c. 74; also, see above.

Triste España sin ventura

llo - rar; Des - po - bla - da d'a -

- le - gri - a, Pa - ra

nun - ca en ti _____ tor - nar!

27

WILLIAM CORNYSHE (d. 1523)

Blow thy horne hunter

William Cornyshe, composer, poet, playwright, and actor, began his career as a singer in the chapel of Henry VII, and eventually rose to become a gentleman of the chapel royal and master of the children. His theatrical and musical talents were happily combined in the various plays and pageants given at court. His court career continued under Henry VIII, who, himself a composer and musician of notable ability, favored Cornyshe very highly and twice took him to France as director of the royal chapel. Among Cornyshe's works are sacred compositions and instrumental dances as well as part songs.

Toward the end of the fifteenth century, French and Italian influences combined with the English popular tradition to produce a new style of composition, the part song. These pieces, usually *a 3,* have a clearly organized song melody in the highest voice, with the lower parts providing a more-or-less chordal harmonization. The exuberant and racy *Blow thy horne hunter* is one of ten part-songs by Cornyshe included in the large "Henry VIII" manuscript,[1] compiled before 1520, during the earlier and happier part of that monarch's reign. Cornyshe puts the popular Tudor tune in the tenor, adding his own much more distinctive top voice. In this "forester song," the singer, in the most thinly disguised way, first boasts of his virility and then deplores his incapacity.

This song happily lends itself to a wide variety of performance possibilities. The apparent problem of eight repetitions (the complete text is given below) can be turned to good advantage if the performance includes a variety of scorings. In a more serious piece, such an approach could seem exaggerated and self-conscious. But in this shamelessly fun-loving song, different scorings, coming in rapid succession, can be fully in keeping with its spirit of joyous mayhem. A male choir of countertenors, tenors, and basses would be ideal, with some verses sung by solo voices; performance by mixed voices is perfectly suitable as well. A wide assortment of instrumental doublings is possible. With solo voices or a small vocal ensemble, recorders, viols, krummhorns, lute, portative organ, and regal are all suitable. With a larger number of singers, cornett, shawms, and sackbuts are very effective, though soft instruments for alternate scorings in a few verses should be used. Some verses can be sung without instruments, and one or two might have only the top voice or tenor sung, with the other parts played. Also, in one or two verses, either the top or lowest part can be omitted entirely, though returning for the refrain.

SOURCE: British Museum, Add. Ms. 31922, fols. 39'–40.
MODERN EDITION: *An English Songbook;* ed. N. Greenberg, New York, 1961, pp. 88 f.

---

[1] The manuscript is so called because of the dozen pieces it contains that are attributed to the king.

REMAINING STANZAS:
Sore this dere strykyn ys and yet she bled no whytt,

she lay so fayre, I cowde nott mys, lord I was glad of it.
　　Now blow thy horne hunter
　　and blow thy horne joly hunter.

As I stod under a banke the dere shoffe [2] on the mede,
I stroke her so that downe she sanke, but yet she was not dede.
　　Now blow thy horne . . .

Ther she gothe, se ye nott, how she gothe over the playne,
And yf ye lust to have a shott, I warrant her barrayne.
　　Now blow thy horne . . .

He to go and I to go but he ran fast a fore,
I had hym shott and strik the do for I myght shott no more.
　　Now blow thy horne hunter

To the covert bothe thay went, for I fownd wher she lay,
An arrow in her hanch she hent,[3] for faynte she myght nott bray.
　　Now blow thy horne . . .

I was wery of the game, I went to tavern to drynk,
now the construcyon on the same, what do yow meane or thynk.
　　Now blow thy horne . . .

Here I leve and mak an end now of this hunter lore,
I thynk his bow ys well unbent, hys bolt may fle no more.
　　Now blow thy horne . . .

PERFORMANCE SUGGESTIONS: ♩ = c. 108; also, see above.
　MODERN SCORING: flute for recorders, oboe or English horn for krummhorns, cornett, or shawms; bassoon or trombone for sackbuts; viola or cello for viols.

---

[2] Pushed.
[3] Caught.

Blow thy horne hunter

PART IV ∾

INSTRUMENTAL MUSIC

Literature and art assure us that instruments played a vital role in the music making of the Middle Ages and the Renaissance. For example, instruments were absolutely essential to the performance of the chanson repertoire of the fifteenth century, and throughout that century vocal music was performed on innumerable occasions by instruments alone. The fact that so little purely instrumental music survives, however, leads us to conclude that much of this music, never written down, was either improvised or was passed on by oral tradition. Aside from some late fifteenth-century pieces for instrumental ensemble, notably by Isaac, the only truly instrumental music of that century that survives is organ music found in various German collections.

From the Middle Ages on, dancing, like music, was an essential part of aristocratic life, and the dancing master was just as highly valued a member of princely households as were the instrumentalists and chapel singers. With the Renaissance, an ever-increasing variety of dances appeared, and were later published in what must have been simple, "lead sheet" form. In fact, many of these dances were the publishers' own

stock "dance band" arrangements of well-known chansons.

It was not until the turn of the sixteenth century that music conceived in the idiom of a particular instrument began to appear in any quantity. Though the vocal connection was still apparent in the chanson transcriptions, many other works were completely original, with no vocal models whatever. The first of a long succession of Italian solo-lute books was followed by keyboard collections and then by music for solo viol and keyboard as well as by instrumental-ensemble music and liturgical organ pieces. All of this music, now printed, found eager players among the rapidly growing numbers of good amateur musicians. A variety of new musical forms arose, with many novel features resulting directly from the idiomatic possibilities inherent in the instruments.

Henceforth, instrument and voice were to develop independently of one another, for the player was no longer compelled to borrow much of his repertoire from the singer. The continually evolving instruments could now boast a repertoire of their own, one which would eventually include some of the greatest music of all time.

28

ANONYMOUS (c. 1480)

Die Katzen Pfote

Germany, which contributed so enormously to music in later centuries, made a late start in native Renaissance music. Though the medieval minnesingers produced an important repertoire, their music was strongly influenced by the French troubadours and trouvères. It was not until the second half of the fifteenth century that any substantial amount of native German music appeared, compiled in three collections known as the *Lochamer*, the *Schedel*, and the *Glogau* songbooks. The last, better known as the *Glogauer Liederbuch*, is the largest and most comprehensive of these, containing 294 pieces, mostly *a 3*. The great bulk of this music was of foreign origin, including many pieces with Latin texts as well as entirely textless compositions by the great Burgundians whose influence extended throughout Europe: Dufay, Ockeghem, Hayne, and Busnois. But scattered throughout the collection are seventy settings of popular German songs. Most of these are love songs in the bar form (AAB) that dates back to the minnesingers, or are through-composed. The pre-existing tunes appeared generally in the tenor, although some do occur as a top voice. The characteristically strong profiles of these German melodies gave to the song settings a unique national flavor of their own. The marriage of the contrapuntal Burgundian style with native elements provided the basis for the great German lieder of the next hundred years.

Die Katzen Pfote (The Cat's Paw) is one of several pieces in the *Glogauer* manuscript that describe a Renaissance "carnival of the animals." (Others are the *Hunter's Horn, Peacock's Dance, Donkey's Crown, Crab's Claw,* and *Crane's Beak*.) This little piece is a perfect illustration of the basic Burgundian two-voice structure, with the two upper parts making a self-sufficient entity. These parts unfold in ever-varying rhythmic complexities (perhaps having some connection with the devious, unpredictable cat). The contratenor is a true bass, jumping awkwardly from note to note and supplying roots freely without being particularly concerned about parallel octaves.

Many scorings are possible. Any of the "families" may be used for whole-consort scorings, but perhaps the more interesting are some of the possible broken-consort scorings. Some of those suggested below are intended to favor somewhat the two upper parts more than the contratenor. The piece may well be played twice, in which case two contrasting scorings are obviously called for. In a twofold performance, one may wish to perform it first as a two-part piece, omitting the contratenor. The adding of this part the second time through gives, as is usual in such a case, a very pleasing cumulative effect. Above all, the performance must have gaiety and brightness.

SOURCE: Berlin Staatsbibliothek, Mus. Ms. 40098, no. 13, fols. 20, 21, 23.
MODERN EDITION: *Das Glogauer Liederbuch, Teil I: Deutsche Lieder und Spielstücke;* ed. H. Ringmann, *Das Erbe deutscher Musik,* Band 4, Kassel, 1954, pp. 94 f.

PERFORMANCE SUGGESTIONS: ♩ = c. 104

I—*Scorings for whole consort:*

S.   soprano or alto recorder
T.   tenor recorder
Ct. bass recorder

or

S.   treble or tenor viol
T.   tenor or bass viol
Ct. bass viol

or

S.   soprano krummhorn
T.   alto krummhorn
Ct. tenor krummhorn

or

S.   cornetto [1]
T.   tenor sackbut
Ct. tenor or bass sackbut

or

S.   soprano shawm [2]
T.   alto shawm
Ct. tenor shawm

I—*Scorings for broken consort:*

S.   soprano or alto recorder
T.   treble viol (an octave higher)
Ct. lute (an octave higher), or soprano krummhorn

or

S.   soprano or alto recorder
T.   tenor recorder
Ct. lute

or

S.   treble viol or soprano krummhorn
T.   tenor viol
Ct. lute

or

S.   treble viol
T.   alto krummhorn
Ct. lute or bass viol

MODERN SCORING:

S.   oboe
T.   English horn
Ct. bassoon

---

[1] Cornetto, shawm and sackbuts may be mixed in any combination.
[2] See n. 1 above.

Die Katzen Pfote

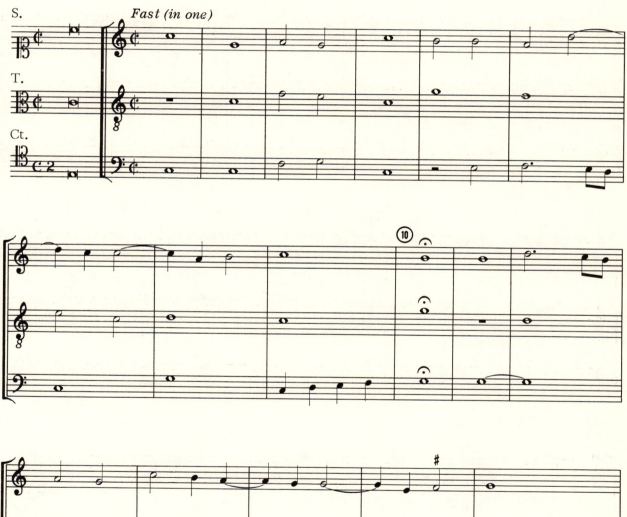

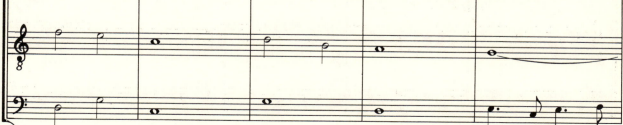

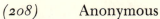

29 ✧

ANTOINE BUSNOIS (d. 1492)

Fortuna desperata

"We must realize," wrote Edward Lowinsky about the ancient Roman goddess of chance, "what part Fortuna plays in Renaissance thought. Innumerable songs of the time sing of her—Italian *frottole,* carnival songs, French *chansons,* English songs. She appears in tablatures and virginal books and even in Masses and motets. The musician was not alone in courting Fortuna. The builders of cathedrals carved her in stone, the painters glorified her power, the poets complained about her caprices, the philosophers tried to penetrate the obscure laws of her rule."[1] "Lady Luck" is clearly her modern descendant.

Busnois's famous song *Fortuna desperata* itself served as the basis for Masses by Obrecht (no. 3) and Josquin, and for numerous chansons, including two by Isaac, as well as later keyboard arrangements. Unlike most of Busnois's other, more progressive chansons (see no. 21), *Fortuna desperata* is very typical of the old Burgundian style. The main melody is in the tenor, and the other two parts move independently. Imitation occurs at only one point in the top voice, in measures 17–21. The contratenor plays its usual mid-fifteenth-century role of filler as well as harmonic bass.

The source used for the present edition is the sixteenth-century "Henry VIII" manuscript (in which twelve pieces are attributed to the king), which gives neither composer nor text for our piece and titles it *Fortune esperée.* There is an added fourth voice, and a *petite reprise* of the last six measures.

Since the principal melody is in the tenor voice, this part may be slightly emphasized in the performance. However, the top voice is melodically as rich as the tenor and equally important, so that an emphasis on the tenor is by no means essential. (Regarding this question, see nos. 28, 30, and 32.) Several "whole" and "broken" scorings are given below. A twofold performance is suggested, using contrasting scorings.

SOURCE: *British Museum Add. Ms. 31922, fols. 4'–5.

MODERN EDITION: Josquin des Prez, *Werken,* ed. A. Smijers, *Wereldlijke werken,* II, ed. A. Antonowycz and A. Elders, Amsterdam, 1965, pp. 25 ff.

PERFORMANCE SUGGESTIONS: ♩ = c. 92

    I—*Whole consort:*
        S.   treble or tenor viol
        T.   bass viol
        Ct.   bass viol
           or
        S.   alto recorder
        T.   tenor recorder
        Ct.   bass recorder

---

[1] E. Lowinsky, "The Goddess Fortuna in Music," *Musical Quarterly,* XXIX (1943), 65.

II—*Broken consort:*
- S.   alto shawm
- T.   tenor sackbut, or tenor or alto shawm
- Ct.   bass or tenor sackbut
    or
- S.   tenor viol
- T.   tenor sackbut
- Ct.   bass viol
    or
- S.   tenor recorder
- T.   bass viol
- Ct.   lute
    or
- S.   alto recorder
- T.   cornetto (played *mp*)
- Ct.   treble viol (an octave higher)
    or
- S.   soprano recorder
- T.   treble viol (an octave higher)
- Ct.   lute

MODERN SCORING:
- S.   oboe
- T.   English horn
- Ct.   bassoon

Fortuna desperata

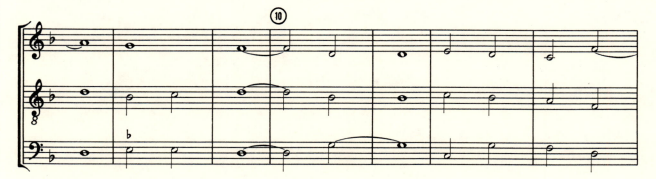

30 ∽

JACOB OBRECHT (c. 1450–1505)

Ic draghe de mutse clutse

Obrecht is the first known composer to have produced a considerable number of purely instrumental pieces. Of his thirty-one secular compositions, seventeen have Dutch titles—a most unusual fact considering both the preference at that time for French and Italian texts for "art" music and the fact that Obrecht spent much of his life abroad, where Dutch was very little known. Perhaps his many Dutch pieces—presumably settings of Dutch popular tunes—simply confirm the fact that, of all the early Flemish masters, he alone was the true Hollander.

Ic draghe de mutse clutse (I wear my cap awry) is one of ten Dutch settings found in the imposing Segovia Cathedral manuscript. No texts are included with these songs; only their Dutch titles are given. In this song, the tenor part is clearly the bearer of the jolly tune—probably a Dutch folk song. Without being able to compare the tune to another source, it is hard to know where quotation of the tune leaves off and musical manipulation—for which Obrecht had a decided liking—begins. Rather than state the tune in what probably was its straightforward original form, he has chosen a varied pattern involving alternations of duos and parlando chordal sec-

tions, twice moving in and out of sections in quick triple meter. Imitation and motivic play are the basis of the duos. Beginning in measure 47, the diminution of the opening phrase of the song enlivens the entire second half of the piece. A similar treatment is found in the same composer's well-known *Tsaat een meskin*,[1] where, after the first section has presented the complete tune in the tenor part, a sort of free fantasia develops material from the first section. This developmental approach is as characteristic of Obrecht's chansons as canonic treatment is of Josquin's.

Another distinctive trait of Obrecht's music is its strong tonal feeling. Here, as in the *Missa Fortuna desperata* (no. 3), there is the almost uninterrupted, resounding F major of the transposed Ionian mode. With only two cadences on a tone other than F, *Ic draghe* asserts its tonic in the strongest possible way and without a trace of monotony.

Several suggested scorings are given below. The bright, pungent character of the piece makes it especially effective for loud winds. A twofold performance, with contrasting scorings, is suggested.

SOURCE: Segovia, Cathedral Ms., fols. 131′–132.
MODERN EDITION: *Van Ockeghem tot Sweelinck,* ed. A. Smijers, III, Amsterdam, 1952, pp. 89 ff.
PERFORMANCE SUGGESTIONS: ♩ = c. 104
    S.   cornetto, treble shawm, or alto shawm
    A.   alto shawm (or tenor sackbut)
    T.   tenor sackbut (or tenor shawm)
    B.   bass sackbut
      or

---

[1] A. T. Davison and W. Apel, eds., *Historical Anthology of Music,* 2 vols., Cambridge, Mass., 1949, I, no. 78, pp. 82–83.

- S.   soprano krummhorn
- A.   alto krummhorn
- T.   tenor krummhorn, or bass viol and lute
- B.   bass krummhorn or regal
  or
- S.   alto recorder
- A.   tenor recorder
- T.   cornetto (an octave higher, *mp*)
- B.   bass recorder and lute
  or
- S.   alto recorder
- A.   tenor recorder
- T.   tenor recorder and lute
- B.   bass recorder

Transposed a tone higher:
- S.   soprano recorder
- A.   alto recorder
- T.   tenor recorder
- B.   bass recorder

MODERN SCORING:
- S.   oboe
- A.   English horn
- T.   trombone
- B.   bassoon

Ic draghe de mutse clutse

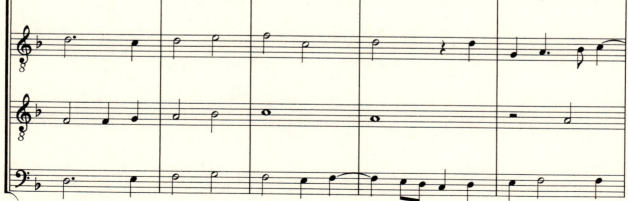

31 〰

ALEXANDER AGRICOLA (c. 1446–1506)

Je n'ay dueil

The early life of Alexander Agricola, like that of so many Renaissance masters, remains largely a question mark. He was born around 1446, probably in Flanders (though perhaps in Germany), and is conjectured to have been a pupil of Ockeghem. His later life alternates, again like so many of his contemporaries, between Italy and the north. He worked for Lorenzo the Magnificent in Florence (where Isaac was a colleague) and for Galeazzo Maria Sforza in Milan as well as in Mantua. Among his northern patrons was Charles VIII, in whose royal chapel he sang, and the Burgundian Philip the Handsome, at whose court Agricola spent the last part of his life.

Agricola's output comprises nine Masses, two Credos, and twenty-five motets, as well as more than ninety secular pieces. His great popularity in his own day is clear from his generous representation in contemporary sources. The motet *Si dedero* is found in no less than nineteen different sources, and Petrucci, a shrewd and successful publisher who knew his clientele, printed nineteen of Agricola's secular pieces and five Masses. *Je n'ay dueil* survives in fourteen sources, of which the most famous is Petrucci's *Odhecaton* (1501).

The opening motive, stated imitatively by each part in turn, consists of the first six notes of the bass part of Ockeghem's chanson of the same name. A shortened version of this motive recurs many times throughout the work (especially in mm. 35–64), making it in effect a kind of fantasia on that motive. However, this is the only connection with Ockeghem's piece; in all other respects, Agricola's song is entirely new.

The text of *Je n'ay dueil* is a *bergerette*, producing the musical form ABBAA (see no. 21). The music is given here without text, as were almost all the pieces in Petrucci's secular collections. Although, of course, there can be no argument about the appropriateness of this piece for vocal performance, we have chosen to present it here textless, as a piece especially suited for viol consort. Such wholehearted instrumental treatment of certain pieces originally composed for voices may well represent the first step in the growing development of an idiomatic instrumental style in the early sixteenth century. (See Helen Hewitt's edition of Petrucci's *Odhecaton* [cited below] for a detailed discussion of the performance implications of untexted vocal pieces and a texted version of this piece.) With the text omitted, the ABBAA form of the piece can be shortened to an ABA form, as it is presented in this score.

SOURCE: *Harmonice musices Odhecaton A,* Petrucci, Venice, 1501, fols. 42'–44.

MODERN EDITION: **Harmonice musices Odhecaton A,* ed. H. Hewitt, Cambridge, Mass., 1942, pp. 302 ff.

PERFORMANCE SUGGESTIONS: ♩ = c. 72
  S. tenor or treble viol
  A. tenor or bass viol
  T. bass viol
  B. bass viol

Je n'ay dueil

Fine

D.C.

32

LOYSET COMPÈRE (c. 1450–1518)

Alons fere nos barbes

Born around 1450, Loyset Compère was a choir-boy at St. Quentin Cathedral. Like Josquin, he was in the service of Galeazzo Sforza, duke of Milan, and in 1486 became *chantre ordinaire* to Charles VIII in Paris, where Ockeghem was his colleague. Later he was appointed canon and chancellor of St. Quentin, where he died in 1518. He was highly regarded both during his own lifetime and afterward, and was the most heavily represented composer in Petrucci's famous *Odhecaton* (1501), with sixteen pieces.

Although he composed a considerable number of sacred works, it is in the chanson that he most excelled. Because many of his chansons are composed in the old *formes fixes,* they seem, on the one hand, old-fashioned. But many of the lighter ones, free of the old forms, have features that mark them as forerunners of the chansons of the 1530s (see no. 34). Lively, saucy texts are handled in a syllabic and eminently singable manner. Lightly conceived points of imitation, alternating with syllabic chordal passages, give these songs their airy, lyric, and sparkling qualities.

Alons fere nos barbes illustrates these features; moreover, it exemplifies the type of chanson based on folk or popular songs. Here, the jaunty tune is divided between the tenor and soprano,

as follows: tenor, measures 4–11; soprano, measures 12–17; tenor, measures 18–23; soprano, measures 31–42. Compère, like his contemporaries, is fond of constantly sharing bits of the tune imitatively among all the voice parts, as, for example, the anticipatory imitation of the beginning of the tune by the alto and bass (mm. 1–3) and the first two phrases of the tune by the soprano (mm. 1–8). In Compère's hands, this highly imitative style becomes particularly transparent. Changes of texture make the ABA form of the piece very clear; the opening and closing strains are presented first imitatively and then homophonically, while the middle strain consists of two duos.

The text survives in corrupt and Italianized versions. Its theme, that of the French lady barber, was evidently a well-known one. The chanson is presented here as it was by Petrucci, without text; but the text is given below to suggest the original flavor. The autonomous musical structure of this chanson and its rhythmic verve make it an attractive instrumental piece. Performance is equally effective for loud or soft instruments; several scorings are recommended below. A twofold performance, with contrasting scorings, would be welcome.

SOURCE: *Harmonice musices Odhecaton A,* Petrucci, Venice, 1501, fols. 28′–29.
MODERN EDITION: **Harmonice musices Odhecaton A,* ed. H. Hewitt, Cambridge, Mass., 1942, pp. 275 f.

TEXT:
Alons fere nos barbes, allons gentil galans!
La barbiere les moglie sovent dos à la foes,
Quant son mari revient de fere sa besogne,

Il trove ses mignons chi luy font vigliecome,
Disant coment va,
Coment fet votre feme,
Fet-elle plus cela?

TRANSLATION:

Let's get our beards done, lads, done:
The lady barber will wet more than one.
The husband back from his business
Finds those who kept busy his missis
Saying: "How's things?
How's the wife?
Still having fun?"

PERFORMANCE SUGGESTIONS: ♩ = c. 104

 S. cornetto or treble shawm
 A. alto shawm
 T. tenor sackbut (or alto shawm)
 B. bass or tenor sackbut
  or
 S. treble viol
 A. tenor or bass viol
 T. tenor or bass viol
 B. bass viol
  or
 S. treble viol
 A. bass recorder
 T. tenor or bass viol
 B. lute
  or
 S. soprano krummhorn
 A. alto krummhorn or regal
 T. alto krummhorn
 B. regal or bass viol
  or
 S. alto recorder
 A. tenor recorder
 T. tenor recorder
 B. bass recorder

MODERN SCORING:

 S. oboe
 A. English horn
 T. English horn
 B. bassoon

Alons fere nos barbes

33

JOANAMBROSIO DALZA (fl. c. 1500)

Tastar de corde con li soi recercar dietro,
Pavana alla ferrarese

If Renaissance vocal music was born in the north, the new instrumental music was now clearly springing from native Italian virtuosi. Petrucci's *Intabulatura de Lauto* of 1507 and 1508, the oldest printed collection of solo instrumental music and the first of a long series of Italian lute books (see no. 25), marked three separate historic milestones.

First of all, these volumes contain lute arrangements of vocal music (rather than merely the original vocal pieces written out in lute tablature), as well as dances and purely instrumental pieces that are independent of either text or dance structure. Simple though these pieces are, they stand clearly at the threshold of the whole new world of independent instrumental music, for they were conceived to explore the unique idiomatic possibilities of a particular instrument. This repertoire set the pattern for the entire sixteenth century.

Book IV in Petrucci's series is by the Milanese lutenist Joanambrosio Dalza. Four of his pieces have the designation *Tastar de corde con li soi recercar dietro* (touching the strings with the *ricercar* following); one of these is included here as no. 33a. The opening section is a purely improvisatory warm-up using simple chords and scales and culminating in a brilliant run that leads directly into the "ricercar following," which is somewhat more organized than the opening. (Dalza's use of the term *ricercar* has no connection with this term's later, more common meaning.)

Dalza's treatment of the dances (*pavanas, saltarellos,* and *pivas*) contained in this volume con-stitutes two other historic landmarks. He did not compile his dance groups at random, but specified their arrangement: "Each *pavana* has its *saltarello* and *piva*." This combination of dances into specified slow-fast sets was the beginning of the whole development of the dance suite. The *pavana,* a slow processional dance of Italian origin, quickly became a very popular court dance and spread throughout Europe. (As the pavan, coupled with the quick galliard, it reached its brilliant climax almost a century later, with the Elizabethan composers.)

The *pavanas* in this collection are variation pieces as well as dances. The Venetian *pavanas* present a single strain followed by a succession of variations on it, while in the Ferrarese *pavanas,* each of several short strains is followed by a varied repeat. Dalza's last *pavana ferrarese* falls into this accepted pattern; each of the three larger sections consists of several strains with varied repetitions. The last section comprises a total of five variations on the same four-measure bass that has already appeared earlier in the piece. In its modest way, this dance is among the first examples of the principle of ground-bass variation, which reached its peak in the gigantic masterworks of the Baroque two hundred years later.

A brief explanation of Italian lute tablature may be interesting at this point. It is a finger notation rather than a pitch notation. The six lines represent the lute's six courses, the lowest being on top (see Plate 9). The numbers refer to the frets that the fingers of the left hand are to stop—o meaning the open string, 1 the first fret (producing a pitch one-half step higher than the open string), 2 the second fret, etc. Rhythmic values are indicated by the various signs placed over the grid, shown here with their corresponding modern staff notation equivalents.

These pieces are playable on the guitar or the harpsichord as well as on the lute. However, warning must be given about playing *any* lute music on keyboard instruments. Every instrument has its own unique qualities and idiosyncracies.

On the lute, even these seemingly simple pieces have certain innate difficulties, which provide a kind of "resistance." The instant such pieces are transplanted to the vastly different idiom of the keyboard, this resistance vanishes and the music then seems dull or too simple. This problem would arise in the same way if one were to play, for example, Bach's unaccompanied violin music on the keyboard.

SOURCE: *Intabulatura de Lauto, Libro Quarto . . . Joanambrosio [Dalza],* Petrucci, Venice, 1508, fols. 6, 21–22.

MODERN EDITION: *Die Tabulatur,* VI–VIII, ed. H. Monkmeyer, Hofheim an Taunus, 1967, pp. 10 f.

PERFORMANCE SUGGESTIONS: see above.

Tastar de corde con li soi recercar dietro

Lute tuning

* 𝄢 𝅝   in original

Finis seguita il recercar

With motion

Pavana alla ferrarese

* in original.

34

MARCO ANTONIO CAVAZZONI (b. c. 1490)

Madame vous aves mon cuer

Pierre Attaingnant, the great music printer in Paris, published his first collection of chansons in 1528, and during the next decade issued another thirty-five songbooks containing well over fifteen hundred chansons. This staggering accumulation reflects the enormous popularity of the new Parisian chansons by such composers as Clément Janequin, Claudin de Sermisy, and Pierre Certon. Though this new generation was trained in the prevailing Flemish style, they modified it to produce a new style of chanson that was truly French. The imitative technique of the contemporary motet served as the underpinnings. But songlike motives using repeated notes, quicker and more pungent rhythms, contrasting imitative and chordal textures, sectional construction, and sometimes the repetition of a short section for another line of text combined to give these songs a hitherto unheard-of sparkle, transparency, and —above all—clarity.

In Italy, these new chansons were immensely popular, and many of them soon appeared in keyboard and lute adaptations by Italian composers. But the Italians then went one step beyond the French, and began composing original keyboard pieces in the new style. Like the French songs, these pieces had great clarity of texture, lively rhythms, variety of treatment, and a clear sectional structure often including repetition. The Italians called these new-style keyboard pieces *canzone francese,* or simply *canzone.* Thus began the long history of the instrumental *canzona,* which in turn paved the way for the sonata and fugue.

Among the first Italian composers to write key-board pieces in this style was Marco Antonio Cavazzoni, born in Bologna (or possibly Urbino) around 1490. He served such influential patrons as Cardinal Bembo and Pope Leo X, and was a singer at St. Mark's in Venice during Willaert's tenure as *maestro di cappella.* His son Girolamo, a pupil of Willaert, was also destined to become an important composer, particularly of *ricercari, alternatim* organ Masses, and Magnificats. The only music by Marco Antonio that survives are the eight keyboard pieces that comprise his *Recerchari, motetti, canzoni, Libro I,* printed in Venice in 1523 by Bernard de Vercelli. Four of these are chanson transcriptions. Although Marco Antonio's *Libro I* slightly predates the publication of the newer French songs, it is generally agreed that the new style features are already reflected in some chansons by the older generation such as Compère, Mouton, and Févin (see no. 32). Among this group must have been the composer—still unidentified—of *Madame vous aves mon cuer.*

The ABA–coda form of this chanson, along with its numerous repetitions of single phrases, its clear chord progressions and cadences, and its interesting tonal plan all undoubtedly mirror the original vocal piece. Though retaining these basic elements, Cavazzoni's transcription replaces the original four-voice vocal texture with a free, idiomatic keyboard style. The essence of this style lies in the freest mixing of chordal writing with simple, independent motion. Several short, characteristic motives recur throughout the piece, providing a unifying element. These are the eighth-note figure in measure 3, the quarter-note figure in measure 9, and the eighth-note figure in measure 16. But perhaps the two most significant aspects of this style are the many written-out ornaments and the complete freedom as to the number of voices present. In their way, these features foreshadow the entire future development of keyboard music.

Performance of this *canzona* is equally effective on the organ or harpsichord. On the organ, the registration must not be too assertive: 8-ft. and 4-ft., or 8-ft. and 2-ft. will prove best. Cavazzoni's piece is highly improvisational in character, and therefore must be performed with freedom and flexibility. This is particularly true of the ornaments; they must not sound mechanical. The performance should sound as if the player himself is improvising and inventing the various ideas as he goes along.

SOURCE: Marco Antonio Cavazzoni, *Recerchari, motetti, canzoni, Libro I,* Vercelli, Venice, 1523, fols. 25′–29.

MODERN EDITION: **Die italienische Orgelmusik am Anfang des Cinquecento,* ed. K. Jeppesen, 2nd ed., Copenhagen, 1960, II, p. 41.

PERFORMANCE SUGGESTIONS: see above.

Madame vous aves mon cuer

Flowing halves

Marco Antonio Cavazzoni

PART V ∿

GENRE AND OCCASIONAL MUSIC

The court composer was one of the most highly valued members of a Renaissance monarch's establishment, and the best composers were among the most sought-after people in all Europe. While it was clear that the resident composer was expected to produce new music as needed—and in that sense was merely an employee, a very high-class servant—his creative ability was nevertheless encouraged to its fullest. Most of the great Renaissance patrons had a genuine love for the arts and, in some cases, were very capable amateur performers themselves; their court composers, artists, and poets were the jewels in their crowns.

Because music played such an important role in Renaissance society, a composer would naturally respond to a momentous occasion with a new piece marking the event, whether a military victory, a royal wedding, or the death of a great person. And the "great persons" thus commemorated were not the composer's royal employers alone, for among the most moving of all occasional pieces are the *déplorations* lamenting the deaths of beloved fellow musicians.

Future generations of composers continued to produce occasional works. The birthday, coronation, and funeral music of Purcell, Handel, and Bach are Baroque examples, and even in the *Academic Festival Overture* of Brahms we see the threads of the still-living tradition.

35

GUILLAUME DUFAY (c. 1400–1474)

Supremum est mortalibus

Some of Dufay's finest compositions are motets, including several ceremonial pieces written specifically to mark important political or historic events. Such an occasion might be the dedication of the cathedral of Florence, the election of a pope, the fall of Constantinople, a royal wedding, or, as in the case of *Supremum est mortalibus,* the signing of a peace treaty. In the spring of 1433, a trouble-ridden Pope Eugene IV, soon to be driven into exile, and an ambitious King Sigismund of Hungary reconciled their political differences and signed a treaty at Viterbo; six weeks later Sigismund was crowned Holy Roman Emperor. In his motet composed to celebrate this event, Dufay set a text in praise of peace written especially for the occasion.

As in much of his music, the top voice in this piece (*triplum*) is the richest part melodically. This part, together with the somewhat less ornamented *motetus,* carries the complete text. The untexted instrumental tenor part is isorhythmic, thus retaining a structural technique long in use during the *Ars nova.* In this technique, the rhythmic and melodic aspects of a musical line were treated separately. The extent of the isorhythmic treatment often varied considerably from piece to piece; though it invariably controlled the tenor part in pieces where it was present, some of the most complex *Ars nova* pieces were isorhythmic in all the voice parts. In *Supremum* (in which only the tenor is isorhythmic), the long tenor melody—called *color*— (mm. 21–104) is divided into three equal segments. Each segment, though a continuation of the melodic line, repeats the sequence of time values

(*talea*) of the first segment. (Each new beginning of the *talea* is indicated in our score by a Roman numeral.) The strict rhythmic order which is thus imposed on the melody extends even to the identical length of rest between segments. Dufay repeats the entire process, beginning at measure 111 with the second statement of the *color;* but this time, because of the new mensural sign, the three statements of the *talea* move twice as fast as before. (Such a diminution of the *talea* was common in isorhythmic motets of the fourteenth century.) At the return to the original time signature (m. 156), the tenor breaks out of its isorhythmic pattern. A text is now added, quoting the beginning of a Magnificat antiphon: "These are the two olive branches."[1] Having become a vocal part, the tenor then joins in the striking fermata-marked chords dramatically acclaiming Eugene and Sigismund, and, at the very end, shares in the last phrase of the "Amen." The two changes of meter also mark the two brief but important moments of melodic return in the otherwise through-composed form.

At certain points in the piece, though never when the tenor is present, Dufay adds the indication "faulxbourdon" (commonly spelled *fauxbourdon*) in the *triplum.* The only voice parts actually notated in these passages are the *triplum* and the *motetus; fauxbourdon* indicates that a third part is to be realized by duplicating every note of the *triplum* a fourth lower. Since the *triplum* and *motetus* move much of the time in

---

1 *Liber Usualis,* Tournai, 1963, p. 1510, from Second Vespers for the Feast of Saints John and Paul, Martyrs.

parallel sixths, the added *fauxbourdon* part converts such passages into chains of parallel $\frac{6}{3}$ chords, creating a sonority different from any other. In this respect as well, Dufay drew on the past for this motet, for English composers before him had discovered and made use of this sonority. Its smooth and euphonious quality makes it especially appropriate for a motet whose text so beautifully describes the state of peace. Because of their textural contrast to the contrapuntal writing in the rest of the piece, the *fauxbourdon* passages also serve to articulate the overall form. Unlike the ever-present *triplum* and *motetus,* the *fauxbourdon* and tenor are never present at the same time; this four-part piece, therefore, actually sounds *a 3.*

The *motetus* and tenor have a signature of B flat, while the *triplum* has none; this is one of many examples in early Renaissance music of a "mixed" or "partial" signature. Works in this category have caused much controversy among present-day scholars,[2] not to mention the performers who must deal head-on with all such problems. Since all five sources for *Supremum* agree in giving the *triplum* no signature, we cannot regard this lack as an oversight to be "corrected" by wholesale editorial addition of B flats. Such a "correction," in any event, would transform Dufay's subtle tonal interplay into a mild G minor. In our edition, we have added only those B flats necessary to avoid tritones and disturbing cross relations (B flat in the *motetus* or tenor coming just before or after a B natural in the *triplum*); otherwise, the B naturals have been left unchanged. Our use of *musica ficta* also includes the typical Burgundian double leading tones at cadences, in accordance with present knowledge of the practice of that period.

Regarding the performance of *Supremum,* one question must be settled at the outset: Are the six untexted passages (such as mm. 15–20 and 59–65) to be sung—that is, are they to be treated as vocal melismas by simply extending the final syllable of text—or are they to be performed instrumentally? (Comparable untexted passages, sometimes very florid, occur in many of Dufay's chansons.) Our present knowledge of Burgundian performance practice does not permit a final

answer to this question, though in many cases instrumental treatment of these passages seems completely convincing. We suggest instrumental performance, which sets off these passages as brief interludes punctuating the otherwise very continuous vocal texture of the work. It follows that the instruments will play also *with* the voices, and not merely during the interludes. The striking effect of the *fermata* chords, however, is most fully realized if they are sung *a cappella,* with instruments resuming at the "Amen."

Viols or organ are suitable instruments. Because the instrumental tenor is a *cantus firmus* and therefore structurally a different type of part, it must have a contrasting timbre: tenor sackbut is ideal. Organ is also suitable, provided a rather bright and distinctive registration is used; but since the tenor is a relatively static part, care must be taken that it not be too loud.

The vocal scoring calls for sopranos or mezzo-sopranos on the *triplum,* countertenors or altos on the *fauxbourdon,* and tenors on the *motetus.* Baritones should sing the texted tenor part at "Isti sunt" (mm. 156–167), and at the *fermata* chords tenors and baritones should exchange parts. Tenors return to the *motetus* at the "Amen," and baritones take the tenor line when it reappears at measure 185. From four to ten voices on a part may be used.

The performance of this work requires great intensity, with the many long phrases well supported and shaped. In addition, the ornamented passages in the *triplum* must have great clarity and agility, without losing the underlying gracefulness of the line.

The new meter at measure 111, transcribed here as $\frac{6}{4}$, is one of the many examples, common in this period, of a proportional tempo relationship. In this instance, one measure of the new $\frac{6}{4}$ fills the same length of time as a measure of the earlier $\frac{3}{4}$. However, in certain Renaissance pieces such tempo relationships cannot be observed literally, for they cause either one tempo to be too slow or the other to be too fast. The only solution in these cases is to regard the change of tempo as relative. *Supremum* is such a case, for if one takes the $\frac{3}{4}$ at ♩ = 126, then the $\frac{6}{4}$ gives ♩. = 84, which is much too fast for this section. The $\frac{6}{4}$ can go no faster than about ♩. = 70. Such a solution observes at least the spirit, if not the letter, of the law, since even at this temp the $\frac{6}{4}$ will still move decidedly faster than the $\frac{3}{4}$. Even more fundamental than the quickening of tempo is the change in

2 Two principal viewpoints are contained in: E. Lowinsky, "The Function of Conflicting Signatures in Early Polyphonic Music," *Musical Quarterly,* XXXI (1945), 227 ff.; and W. Apel, "The Partial Signatures in the Sources up to 1450," *Acta Musicologica,* X (1938), 1 ff.; XI (1939), 40 ff.

the kind of meter, simple triple meter changing to compound duple meter. Because of this, the performance at the $\frac{6}{4}$ must have a brighter vocal sound and a more animated rhythmic quality. The *fermata*-chord passage is perhaps most effective if it is sung not only *a cappella,* but more softly than the rest of the piece, and without vibrato or expression. The opening tempo returns with the first meter at the "Amen." Through the judicious use of subtly contrasting dynamic levels in the various smaller divisions of the piece, a well-articulated form will emerge.

SOURCE: Trent Cod. 92, fols. 22'–24.

MODERN EDITION: *Denkmäler der Tonkunst in Österreich,* Jahrg. XL, Band 76, pp. 24 f.

TRANSLATION:

The supreme good of mankind is peace, the highest God's best gift. In time of true peace, the law's excellence and the constancy of justice flourish. In peace the day is passed in joy and the night in tranquil sleep. Peace teaches the maiden to adorn her tresses with gold and to do up her hair. In peace, the streams and birds sing in praise, and the hills lie open, happy and pleasant. In peace the rich traveler moves safely; the plowman dwells secure in the land.

O holy peace, so long awaited, so sweet and pleasing to man! May you be eternal and steadfast without deceit; rejoice that faith is always with you. And may those who granted you to us, O peace, reign without end. Let our Eugenius be pope and Sigismund be king forever.   Amen.

Tenor: They are two olive branches.

PERFORMANCE SUGGESTIONS: ♩ = c. 126; at $\frac{6}{4}$, ♩. = c. 70; also, see above.

MODERN SCORING: viola and cello in place of viols; trombone in place of sackbut.

Supremum est mortalibus

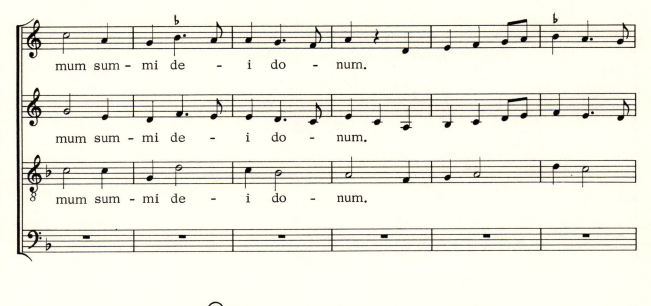

mum sum - mi de - i do - num.

mum sum - mi de - i do - num.

mum sum - mi de - i do - num.

Pa - ce ___ ve - ro

Pa - ce ___ ve - ro le -

T. I

le - gum pre - stan - ci - a vi - get at - que re -

gum pre - stan - ci - a ___ vi -

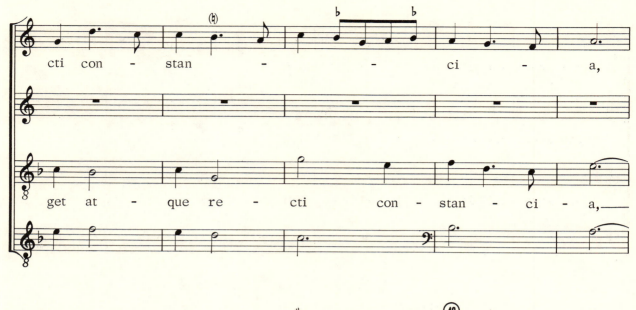

cti con - stan - - - ci - a,

get at - que re - cti con - stan - ci - a, ___

pa - ce di - es so - lu - tus et

___ pa - ce di - es so - lu - tus ___ et

le - tus, no - cte som - nus tra - hi -

le - tus ___ no - cte som - nus tra -

T. III

T. IV

³ See commentary on pp. 3, 252.

ex - pe - cta - ta mor-ta-li - bus tam

ex - pe - cta - ta, _____ mor-ta-li - bus tam

Faulxbourdon

dul - cis tam gra - ta,

dul - cis tam gra - ta,

sis e - ter - na fir - ma si -

sis _____ e - ter - na fir - ma

T.V

pos - si - de - ant _____

pos - si - de - ant _____ re - gnum

re-gnum si-ne fi - ne:

si - ne fi-ne: _____

Sit no - ster _____ hic _____ pon - ti -

Sit _____ no - ster hic pon - ti -

I - sti _____ sunt du -

36

HEINRICH ISAAC (c. 1450–1517)

Quis dabit capiti meo aquam?

Among the most moving compositions of the Renaissance are settings of lamentations, either taken from Scripture, such as David's lament for Absalom (see no. 14), or composed on the death of a contemporary, such as Josquin's *Déploration* on the death of Ockeghem. The powerful lament *Quis dabit capiti meo aquam,* set to a specially composed Latin text, was Isaac's tribute to Lorenzo de' Medici, who at his death in 1492 was unquestionably the greatest patron of the arts in fifteenth-century Italy. Thus were united in this piece the efforts of Isaac, the highly esteemed court composer to Lorenzo and teacher to Lorenzo's children, and Angelo Poliziano, court poet and literary favorite of Lorenzo's humanist circle.

Quis dabit can be called a fantasia on the final phrase of the antiphon *Salva nos* from Sunday Compline.[1] With the exception of measures 102–120, there is scarcely a moment of the entire work that is not haunted by this fragment (for example, the soprano part at the opening, the bass at m. 9, and the tenor at m. 15).[2] In the third

strophe, (mm. 65–101), this phrase appears in a plain, syllabic version and with the original words "et requiescamus in pace" (and may we rest in peace) restored. Now stated as a *basso ostinato,* it is made more noticeable by the absence of the tenor part, and more stark by its contrast to the florid style of the upper voices. But at the heart of this section are two striking examples of musical symbolism: the indication "laurus tacet" in the silent tenor part refers both to the laurel tree struck down and to the great Lorenzo, silenced by death; and the bass reiteration of "et requiescamus in pace"—in a slowly descending sequence with each statement beginning a tone lower—can only be interpreted as Lorenzo's descent into the grave. But this profoundly sorrowful and austere work never lapses into sentimentality. Its low ranges, Phrygian cadences, open fifths, and above all the sparing use of florid writing—so effectively set off by the longer sustained notes in the other

---

[1] *Liber Usualis,* Tournai, 1963, p. 271. The final phrase of the antiphon is given here for comparison with the motet.

$$ \text{et re - qui - es - ca - mus\_ in\_ pa - ce.} $$

[2] As Martin Staehelin has pointed out in his edition, Heinrich Isaac, *Messen, Band 2,* three portions of *Quis dabit* also appear in the *Missa Salva nos,* which uses the complete Compline antiphon as its *cantus firmus.* But since we do not know the date of composition of this Mass, we can only speculate as to which work was composed first. The fact that *Quis dabit* is so convincing a work from every standpoint strongly suggests that the motet must have been the original version of this music. On the other hand, Isaac

used the complete chant antiphon as the basic structural element of the Mass, running almost continuously through each movement. This fact, as Edward Lerner has pointed out, argues heavily that the Mass, so compellingly structured, must have been the original work. Considering Lorenzo's death and the meaning of the final phrase of the antiphon, it is not too difficult to imagine Isaac "lifting" those portions of the Mass containing this fragment to use as parts of the "new" *Quis dabit.* A further complication is introduced in Allan Atlas's doctoral dissertation ("Rome, Biblioteca Apostolica Vaticana, Capella Giulia XIII.27 and The Dissemination of The Franco-Netherlandish Chanson in Italy," c. 1460–c. 1530, New York University, 1972). He has shown that *Quis dabit,* in the Ms. Cappella Giulia XIII.27, had another text, in praise of St. Cecilia (!), that had been scratched out, but that is visible under ultraviolet light. As Atlas himself remarks, however, logical conclusions have yet to be drawn from this most curious discovery.

voices—all contribute to Isaac's incomparable control, which makes the anguish of the text the more poignant.

Because this work is conceived entirely for vocal sonorities, *a cappella* performance is absolutely essential. The written pitch calls for countertenors or altos, tenors, baritones, and basses, but the choral director should by all means experiment with a slightly higher pitch since this may bring the voice parts into better ranges for his singers. Performance by S.A.T.B. choir is also completely successful, requiring transposition a minor third higher. In any event, transposition must be used only to accommodate singers' ranges, and must not reach the point of giving an unwanted brightness to this darkly colored, brooding work. In the three-voiced middle section, it is strongly recommended that the two upper parts, because of their florid style, be sung by soloists, with the bass "Et requiescamus in pace" statements sung chorally. The bass ostinato then stands vividly apart from the solo voices because of its choral timbre, and is thus made all the more dramatic. The resulting large format of choir–solo–choir also reinforces the work's tripartite form. The vocal quality, the expressive shaping of phrases, the flexibility of tempo, the wide dynamic range—in short, all the aspects of the performance—must be imbued with the intensity of this work.

SOURCE: Florence, Biblioteca Nazionale Centrale II. I, 232 (olim Magl. XIX/58).

MODERN EDITION: *Denkmäler der Tonkunst in Österreich,* Jahrg. XIV/1, Band 28, ed. J. Wolf, pp. 45 f.

TRANSLATION:

Who will give my head water?
Who will give my eyes a fountain
of tears
that I may weep by night,
that I may weep by day?

Thus the bereaved turtledove is wont to mourn,
thus the dying swan,
thus the nightingale.
Woe is me,
O grief!

The laurel struck suddenly by a thunderbolt
lies there;
the laurel, celebrated by choirs
of all the Muses,
by dances of all the nymphs.
    (*bass:* And may we rest in peace.)

Under his spreading shelter
even Phoebus' lyre
sounded more enticingly
and his voice more sweetly.
Now all is silent;
now all is deaf.

PERFORMANCE SUGGESTIONS: ♩ = c. 64; also, see above.

Quis dabit capiti meo aquam?

Secunda pars

Lau - rus im - pe - tu ful - - - -

Lau - rus, *lau - rus* im - pe - tu

Et___ re - qui - e - sca - mus___ in pa -

Tenor Laurus tacet.

- - mi - nis il - la il - la ja -

ful - mi - nis il - la *il - la* ja -

ce, et___ re - qui - e - sca - mus___

- cet su - - - - bi - to, lau -

- - - - cet su - bi - to, lau -

___ in pa - ce, et___

- - - - - - rus___

-

___ re - qui - e - sca - mus___ in pa - ce,

Tertia pars

37

HEINRICH ISAAC (c. 1450–1517)

Donna di dentro

Florence, that jewel of Renaissance Italy, had an annual tradition of carnivals. These preceded Lent and also occurred for a span of several weeks in the early summer. Lorenzo de' Medici (the Magnificent), whose rule in Florence began in 1469, raised these festivals to spectacular new heights. Among the many attractions were torchlight processions of lavishly decorated chariots fitted out with magnificent displays and carrying masked revelers.

Music played a vital role in the carnivals, and a large repertoire of carnival songs (canti carnascialeschi) soon appeared. Lorenzo himself wrote the poetry for some of these. The guilds and trades were among the most popular subjects; thus there were songs of the candlemakers, of the millers, of the perfumers, etc. Some of the songs had political twists. Broad humor characterized most of the texts—many of the songs clearly had double meanings, and some were outright obscene, such as the anonymous song about women hunting for rabbits ("We are all young women who hunt, and we never ask for any other kind of exercise").

Lorenzo died in 1492, and two years later the short but horrendous reign of the monk Savonarola began. Under his fanatic rule, the carnivals became times of solemn religious processions and sermons. On some of these occasions, the entire populace looked on while hundreds of musical instruments and manuscripts of "objectionable" music were destroyed on huge bonfires. Some of the best-known carnival songs—including very obscene ones—were turned into laude (see no. 16) and fitted out with new, penitential texts.

With the execution of Savonarola in 1498, the carnival returned, but in more sober dress than before.

The carnival songs varied greatly in their degree of complexity. Many were in simple, chordal style, similar to the newly developing frottole (see no. 24), using almost exclusively the tonic, subdominant, and dominant chords. They were intended primarily for outdoor performance, and contemporary accounts mention the use of many instruments. Many of the songs were by anonymous composers, but some of the best were written by Heinrich Isaac, international Netherlander par excellence and composer to Lorenzo. Combining the features of the new Italian secular music with the totally different characteristics of his native Flemish style, he produced some of the finest examples of carnival songs. Unfortunately, only a small number of these have survived. (For further comments on the new Italian secular style and its influence on later Renaissance music, see nos. 24 and 25.)

Donna di dentro, Isaac's best-known carnival song, is a quodlibet—that is, a piece that contains several different pre-existent tunes or fragments of tunes. This song brings together snatches of three very popular tunes of the time, combining them in a highly imitative texture and showing the full contrapuntal dazzle of Isaac's Flemish style. The two outer voice parts lie perfectly for sopranos and baritones. The two inner parts, both in tenor range, must be sung either by tenors, or a mixture of countertenors (or altos) and tenors. Cornettos, shawms, and sackbuts are the ideal instruments. Viols—though far less effective for this piece than the winds—can, if necessary, be used instead. Soprano recorder doubling the highest part will give a good added brightness.

This exuberant and rousing piece should be performed in a vibrant, almost boisterous manner.

SOURCE: Florence, Biblioteca Nazionale Centrale II. I (olim Magl. XIX/59).

MODERN EDITION: *Denkmäler der Tonkunst in Österreich,* Jahrg, XIV/1, Band 28, pp. 35 f.

TRANSLATION:

(*Donna, di dentro . . .*)
Lady, in your house are roses, lilies, and blooms.

(*Dammene un pocho . . .*)
Give me a bit of that mazacroca, but not too much.

(*Fortuna d'un gran tempo . . .*)
Fortune for a long time was mine.

PERFORMANCE SUGGESTIONS: $\downarrow$ = c. 104

NUMBER OF VOICES: sixteen to thirty-two.

S.	sopranos	with cornetto or soprano shawm, and soprano recorder
Ct.	countertenors (or altos) and tenors	with tenor sackbut or tenor shawm
T.	countertenors (or altos) and tenors	with alto shawm or tenor or alto sackbut
B.	baritones/basses	with tenor or bass sackbut

MODERN SCORING:

S.	with oboe (or two oboes, depending on the size of the chorus)
Ct.	with trombone
T.	with trombone
B.	with trombone

Donna di dentro

38

HEINRICH ISAAC (c. 1450–1517)

A la bataglia

Through the huge murals recreating victorious battles, the Renaissance rulers who commissioned them were sure that their military successes would be permanently imprinted on the world. Leonardo da Vinci, Michelangelo, and Uccello (see Plate 12) were among the many artists who created these vivid canvases. Theatrical productions of the time also included an occasional battle scene, certainly sure-fire theater. Isaac's *A la bataglia*, the first in a long series of battle pieces, may have been used to accompany such a scene in one of Lorenzo de' Medici's plays; it was apparently composed to celebrate the Florentine victory at Sarzanello in 1487. This early genre of program music continued to attract the fancy of many later composers, including Clément Janequin, William Byrd, and Claudio Monteverdi.

Isaac's piece clearly calls for loud winds. Its sectional form strongly suggests antiphonal scoring (as indicated in the music); this approach also highlights the pictorial element implied by both the title and the repeated short fanfare motives. Colorful and contrasting timbres should be used, but at the same time, the typically Flemish imitative style requires that the four voice parts be played with equal strength. With these thoughts in mind, the following plan is suggested: Ensemble I, comprising four loud winds, will provide the basic sound of the piece. Ensemble II will have a decidedly different color, and will play as the alternate group in some sections. In still other sections, both groups will combine.

Here, as in so many pieces of this period, the top line lies rather low, and both middle parts lie in the tenor register. In order to achieve a brighter and more open sonority for this rousing piece, our scoring for ensemble I transposes the alto part an octave higher (putting it above the soprano); in ensemble II, both middle parts are played an octave higher, and the top part *two* octaves higher, using the piercing brightness of the sopranino recorder. Scorings for the two ensembles are given below.

Percussion, absolutely mandatory in any battle piece, adds a whole new dimension to the performance. Two drums of indefinite pitch but with contrasting sounds (or two timpani tuned to F and C) and a small snare drum would be perfect. The following suggestions serve as a general guide to the percussionist:

(1) The good player will try to enhance the separate rhythmic nature of each section of the piece, which will require a different treatment for each section.

(2) The player must spend his few sonorities very economically. This will mean using only one or the other instrument in some sections.

(3) Within larger sections, let some phrases have no percussion at all while other phrases have only sparing use of percussion. In contrast, some places could well be very "busy."

The percussion part shown in the score is intended only as a guide; obviously more than one realization is possible. From these few points it becomes clear that the percussion part must, at all costs, avoid monotony and, in the true spirit of improvisation, should let itself be caught up in the spontaneity of this rousing, colorful piece.

SOURCE: Florence, Biblioteca Nazionale Centrale, Ms. Panciatichi 27, fol. 9'.

MODERN EDITION: *Denkmäler der Tonkunst in Österreich,* Jahrg. XVI, Teil I, Suppl., ed. J. Wolf, Band 32, pp. 221 ff.

PERFORMANCE SUGGESTIONS: ♩ = c. 104

	ensemble I	*ensemble II*
S.	alto shawm	sopranino recorder
Ct.	soprano shawm	rauschpfeife
T.	tenor sackbut	soprano shawm
B.	bass sackbut	bass viol (with bass krummhorn or regal)
	plus	*plus*
	timpani or drums	snare drum

A la bataglia

1 Percussion parts have been added as suggestions by the editors.

[ENSEMBLE II]

[ENSEMBLE I]

Secunda pars

(o = ♩.) [ENSEMBLE I]

Tertia pars
[ENSEMBLE I] (150)

Heinrich Isaac

[ENSEMBLE II] ⒄

39 ✌

ANONYMOUS (c. 1493)

Viv' el gran Re Don Fernando

The proud and magnificent city of Granada was the last remaining jewel of the great Moorish civilization which had flourished and prospered in Spain for more than seven centuries. Fired by a fierce Christian zeal, the Catholic sovereigns Ferdinand and Isabella determined to wage a holy war to vanquish this last infidel stronghold on Spanish soil. After a bitter struggle lasting nearly ten years, Granada fell to the besieging Spanish armies in 1491.

Several Spanish songs celebrated Ferdinand's Moorish victories. However, as Robert Stevenson has pointed out,[1] these restrained and austere songs certainly do not convey any feeling of rejoicing. Apparently Spanish composers took their cue from Isabella, whose first act after every victory was to summon everyone to pray for the conversion of the vanquished. In striking contrast, Italians hailed the Spanish triumphs in true Latin spirit, complete with bullfights and fireworks.

The anonymous *frottola, Viv' el gran Re Don Fernando,* salutes the fall of Granada with typical Italian exuberance. The first *frottola* ever printed, it was included in a play written to celebrate Spain's final victory, and published at Rome in 1493.[2] It is as simple and artless as an outdoor carnival song, though the short imitative section adds a touch of high-art style with its increased excitement approaching the cadence.

Lying well for S.A.T.B., *Viv' el gran Re* can be performed either by solo voices or small vocal ensemble, with or without instruments in either case. Altos and tenors will need to exchange parts for all of the piece except for measures 7–11. If instruments are used, they should be *tacet* for the middle section (mm. 12–16). This plan nicely articulates the ABA form, and the change of timbre makes the piece all the more colorful. If desired, the piece can very readily be extended; a repeat of the B section after reaching the *fine,* followed by a second *da capo,* will result in the form ABABA. The performance should have a bright, joyous sound and spirited rhythm.

SOURCE: Carlo Verardi, *Historia baetica,* E. Silber, Rome, 1493, fols. 45–46.
MODERN EDITION: *R. Stevenson, *Spanish Music in the Age of Columbus,* The Hague, 1960, p. 248; for a different text setting, see A. Einstein, *The Italian Madrigal,* Princeton, 1949, I, p. 36.

TRANSLATION:
Long live King Ferdinand the Great,
And Queen Isabella!
Long live Spain and Castile,
Full of glory, triumphing!
The Mohammedan city,

---

[1] R. Stevenson, *Spanish Music in the Age of Columbus,* The Hague, 1960, p. 249.
[2] See Plate 13.

Most powerful Granada,
From the false pagan faith
Has been broken and freed
By the valor and armed might
Of Ferdinand and Isabella.
Long live Spain and Castile,
Full of glory, triumphing!

PERFORMANCE SUGGESTIONS: ♩. = c. 70
NUMBER OF VOICES: solo voices, or vocal ensemble of twelve to sixteen voices.

S.	soprano	with soprano krummhorn
A.	tenor (mm. 7–11, alto)	with tenor viol
T.	alto (mm. 7–11, tenor)	with alto krummhorn
B.	bass	with bass viol

MODERN SCORING:

S.	oboe
A.	viola
T.	English horn
B.	cello or bassoon

Viv' el gran Re Don Fernando

40 ❧

JUAN PONCE (fl. 1500)

Ave, color vini clari

Through the centuries, musicians have toasted the delights of wine in drinking songs. This genre has included such pieces as the Renaissance songs for the St. Martin's feast, the rowdy Restoration catches, and the *brindisi* of nineteenth-century Italian opera. A very elegant example is this one by a singer at the court of the Catholic king Ferdinand of Spain. Juan Ponce is known to us by a mere dozen compositions, ten of which are found in the *Cancionero musical de Palacio* (see no. 26). *Ave, color vini clari* is one of the earliest pieces copied into that vast collection. The text, a medieval student drinking song, is a third-hand adaptation of a still older drinker's parody (*Vinum bonum et suave*) of the twelfth-century sequence *Verbum bonum et soave*. The joyous text was set yet again generations later by Lassus, but propriety finally triumphed when that master's sons refitted their father's motet, after his death, with a more seemly pious text,

Ave decus coeli clari—coming full circle in four hundred years!

This work has the appearance of a "take-off" on the conventional motet style—touches of the fashionable pervading imitation; imitation by paired voices; *proportio tripla* (cut time changing to $\frac{3}{4}$, with the duration of each measure remaining the same) at important cadential sections, and passages in chordal style (mm. 31–46). Although the form as a whole is too extended to be classed as a *villancico*, the first seventeen measures return at the close with new text and minor changes, much like the *villancico*'s refrain. The three intervening stanzas have an obvious textural symmetry: the central one is almost purely homorhythmic, while the neighboring strophes feature duos and bits of imitation. The work's major difference from the true motet style is the frequent and complete articulation provided by cadences at the close of each section; another is the return of the opening section.

SOURCE: Madrid, Biblioteca del Palacio Real, *Cancionero musical de palacio*, 2-I-5, fols. 97'–98.

MODERN EDITION: *La Música en la corte de los reyes católicos*, ed. H. Anglès, Monumentos de la música española, Barcelona, 1947, V, pp. 188 ff.

TRANSLATION:

Hail, hue of clear wine, hail savor without equal, your power intoxicates us! O how happy a creation produced by the pure vine; every table is secure in your presence. O how pleasing in color, how fragrant in odor, how tasty to the mouth, the tongue's sweet prison! Happy the belly you enter, happy the throat you moisten, happy the mouth you lave, O blessed lips! Therefore, let us praise wine; let us exalt drinkers and confound abstainers for ever and ever. Amen.

PERFORMANCE SUGGESTIONS: ♩ = c. 84

NUMBER OF VOICES: solo voices or choral ensemble (twelve to thirty voices) *a cappella*.

S. countertenor (or alto)
A. tenor
T. baritone
B. bass

Ave, color vini clari

Juan Ponce

41 ∽

JOSQUIN DES PREZ (c. 1445–1521)

Vive le roy!

The last of Josquin's royal patrons was Louis XII of France, to whose court he came in around 1512 and where he apparently remained until the king's death in 1515. Louis once suggested to Josquin that he write a piece in which the king could sing. Josquin obliged with a piece with one part marked "vox regis." His opinion of the king's vocal ability was clearly not high, since the "king's part" consisted of a single note repeated all the way through. The bass (to be sung by Josquin) alternated between the octave and fifth below the king's part—perhaps to keep the royal note in tune!

More seriously, it is generally assumed that Louis XII is the king Josquin intended to honor with his brilliant fanfare *Vive le roy!* In this "riddle" piece, one of a popular genre of the time, the tenor part was not written out, but had to be discovered by translating the vowels of the French title into solmization syllables (with U substituted for V, as was then customary) as follows:

V	I	V	E	[L]	E	[R]	O	Y
ut	mi	ut	re		re		sol	mi
C	E	C	D		D		G	E

This *soggetto cavato dalle vocale* (subject dug out of the vowels) becomes a *cantus firmus* that Josquin states three times, the second of these transposed down a fourth. The other parts independently pursue a three-voice canon and do not share in the "royal theme," though they make great play with the third, its most characteristic interval. The fanfare motive for the canon is borrowed from an anonymous chanson, *Vive le roy et sa puisanse.*

Petrucci, who printed the piece in 1503 (in *Canti C,* the third installment of his *Odhecaton*), was apparently unwilling to trust the solution of the puzzle to his public, for he printed the "realized" tenor part. But perhaps unable to resist a puzzle of his own, he included a cryptic Latin verse to explain the already-solved musical puzzle. Professor Edward Lowinsky has very kindly made available to us his translation, which we have paraphrased as follows:

> Form the appropriate solmization syllables out of these vernacular words, whence the tenor is derived; it proceeds in unchanging course, except that its second [series] succeeds the first at a fourth below.

Such a puzzle piece may promise to be very pedantic, but that is certainly not the case with *Vive le roy!*, which shows what Josquin's lively imagination could do with even such unpretentious beginnings.

There can be no doubt that Josquin intended this fanfare for cornetts and sackbuts. In the scorings given below, the *cantus firmus* is strengthened by a second instrument.

SOURCE: *Canti C [Odhecaton],* Petrucci, Venice, 1503, fols. 131′–132.

MODERN EDITION: Josquin des Prez, *Werken,* ed. A. Smijers, *Wereldlijke Werken,* II, eds. M. Antonowycz and W. Elders, Amsterdam, 1965, pp. 10 ff.

PERFORMANCE SUGGESTIONS: ♩ = c. 104
- S.   cornett (or soprano shawm)
- Ct.   alto sackbut (or alto shawm)
- T.   two tenor sackbuts, or tenor sackbut and alto or tenor shawm or tenor shawm
- B.   bass sackbut

MODERN SCORING:
- S.   trumpet
- Ct.   trombone
- T.   two trombones
- B.   trombone

Vive le roy!

Glossary

Alternatim setting: a practice common in medieval and Renaissance chant-based sacred music in which polyphonic sections alternated with chant sections.

Ars nova (Lat., new art): refers to fourteenth-century music (contemporary theorists referred to thirteenth-century music as *Ars antiqua*). Ars nova music was chiefly noted for a new variety of rhythms and meters, made possible by a more detailed system of rhythmic notation than had existed before 1320.

Bergerette: see **Formes fixes.**

Bicinium (Lat.)—a two-voiced composition.

Caccia (It., chase)—a fourteenth-century Italian form in strict two-part canon with a free third voice in longer notes; the text frequently described hunting scenes.

Cadence types:

(1) Under-third cadence:

(2) Burgundian cadences or double-leading-tone cadences:

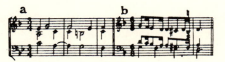

(3) Phrygian cadences:

Cancionero: see **Chansonnier.**

Canonical hours: also called Divine or Holy Office; in the liturgy of the Catholic church, the eight Offices of the hours, as distinct from the Mass. These services included Psalms, antiphons, responsories, hymns, and canticles. Musically the most important of the Offices were Matins (sung during the night), Lauds (at dawn), Vespers (at twilight), and Compline (after Vespers). The complete daily Office was sung only in monastic churches.

Cantus firmus (Lat.): a pre-existing melody which serves as the structural basis for a polyphonic work. The *cantus firmus* is generally placed in the tenor, and is frequently written in longer note values than those of the other parts.

Canzona: an instrumental piece of the sixteenth and seventeenth centuries which developed from the imitative chanson of the earlier sixteenth century. The frequently imitative and sectional *canzona* was the forerunner of the later Baroque forms such as sonata and fugue.

Chace (Fr., chase): a fourteenth-century French form in strict three-part canon. The *chace*, unlike the Italian *caccia*, has no supporting free voice.

Chanson (Fr., song): a polyphonic piece with French text. Most medieval chansons were in one of the **formes fixes** (*q.v.*). The early Renaissance composers retained these, and wrote chiefly *virelais, rondeaux,* and *ballades* for one or two voices and instruments. Later Renaissance composers wrote free-form chansons in an imitative four-part texture; some of these were intended for purely vocal performance.

Chansonnier: a manuscript collection of chansons. Some of these manuscripts were sumptuously decorated. A *cancionero* is the Spanish counterpart of the French *chansonnier*.

Compline responsory: see **Canonical hours.**

Cyclic Mass: a Mass in which similar musical elements, either the same tenor or the same opening motive, recur in all the movements.

Dances: Sixteenth-century instrumental dances were frequently grouped into sets, such as the *pavana, saltarello,* and *piva*. The *pavana* was a slow, dignified dance in $\frac{4}{4}$ meter; the *saltarello* was a faster, triple-meter dance, often simply a quicker variant of the *pavana;* and the *piva,* in $\frac{12}{8}$ or $\frac{6}{8}$, was the fastest of all. The *gagliarda* was a dance similar to the *saltarello*, with frequent alternations between $\frac{3}{4}$ and $\frac{6}{8}$ meters (hemiola). Later in the sixteenth century, the *pavan* and *galliard* were frequently composed as a pair; Elizabethan virginal composers produced some of their greatest music in these forms.

David lament: a musical setting of the lament of David for his beloved son Absalom (2 Samuel 18:33). Several Renaissance composers set this text.

Fauxbourdon (Fr., false bass): in fifteenth-century French music, a practice in which a melodic line was doubled at the sixth below or, at cadences, at the octave. A third, unwritten part was supplied by the singer at the fourth below, resulting in a succession of parallel $\frac{6}{3}$ chords with $\frac{8}{5}$ sonorities at cadences.

Formes fixes (Fr.): the *ballade, virelai,* and *rondeau,* the three forms of fourteenth-century French poetry and secular vocal music. These rigidly patterned forms were gradually replaced in the fifteenth century with various freer forms. The *bergerette* was a one-stanza *virelai*.

Gagliarda: see **Dances.**

Incipit (Lat.): the first words of a text; also sometimes refers to the opening phrase of music.

International Flemish style: the style of Josquin and his contemporaries, characterized by four-voice writing, with equal importance of all the parts, much imitation, and occasional short chordal sections. This style became the international norm at the end of the fifteenth century, when many northern composers took posts throughout Europe, carrying their compositional techniques with them. The Flemish influence remained alive until the death of Lassus at the end of the sixteenth century.

Isorhythm: a system for organizing the tenors (and sometimes other voices) of fourteenth-century motets. The tenors were divided into sections, and an exactly identical rhythmic pattern (called *talea*) was imposed on each section.

Madrigalism: a term for the descriptive word painting common in the madrigals of the later sixteenth century.

Marian antiphons: four chant melodies in honor of the Virgin Mary. During each season of the year, a different Marian antiphon is sung at the end of Compline. The four antiphons are *Alma Redemptoris Mater, Ave Regina caelorum, Regina caeli,* and *Salve, Regina.*

Musica ficta (Lat., false music): the unwritten tradition, well understood by medieval and Renaissance musicians, of adding accidentals to music according to specific principles. Because the practice varied with time and place, the proper method for adding accidentals has been a very controversial subject among modern scholars.

Organ registration: in organ terminology, 8-foot indictates written (unison) pitch, 4-foot sounds an oc-tave above written pitch, 2-foot sounds two octaves above. Several other pitches are also usually found, all indicated in length of feet. This system, long in use, is based on the approximate length of the open pipe sounding the lowest note on the organ keyboard (C two octaves below middle C).

Pavana: see **Dances.**

Piva: see **Dances.**

Psalm tones: the melodic formulas used for singing the Psalms in Gregorian chant. There is both a simple and more elaborate psalm tone for each of the eight church modes.

Quodlibet: a contrapuntal combination of several different tunes or parts of tunes in one piece.

Ricercare (It.): a sixteenth- and seventeenth-century instrumental piece, most commonly in an imitative style like that of the vocal motet. The early sixteenth-century lute *ricercare* was a short piece in a non-imitative free style.

Saltarello: see **Dances.**

Sestina: a poetic form used by Dante and Petrarch in the fourteenth century, containing six six-line stanzas.

Tablature; intabulature: a system of notation for lute or keyboard, in which pitches are indicated by letters or numbers rather than by notes on a staff.

Tactus (Lat., beat): in the Middle Ages and Renaissance, the normal unit of beat.

Vagans (Lat., wanderer): the fifth voice in sixteenth-century polyphonic music. The *vagans* had no established range requirements.

Villancico: In the fifteenth- and sixteenth-centuries, a Spanish poetic and musical form characterized by a recurring refrain between stanzas. Some *villancicos* were in a contrapuntal style, while others were simpler and more chordal.

Virelai: see **Formes fixes.**

A Selected Reading List

Apel, Willi, *The Notation of Polyphonic Music*, Cambridge, 1953.

Bessaraboff, Nicholas, *Ancient European Musical Instruments*, Cambridge, 1941.

Dart, Thurston, *The Interpretation of Music*, London, 1954.

Donington, Robert, "Ornamentation," in *Grove's Dictionary of Music and Musicians*, 5th ed., New York, 1954.

———, *The Interpretation of Early Music*, rev. ed., New York, 1974.

Ganassi, Sylvestro, *Opera Intitulata Fontegara* (1535), ed. Hildemarie Peter, Eng. trans. Dorothy Swainson, Berlin, 1956.

Harrison, F., and J. Ritter, *European Musical Instruments*, London, 1964.

Hewitt, Helen, ed., *Harmonice Musices Odhecaton A* (Venice, 1501), critical commentary, pts. III and IV, Cambridge, 1942.

Horsley, Imogene, "Improvised Embellishments in the Performance of Renaissance Polyphonic Music," *Journal of the American Musicological Society*, IV (1951), 3–19.

Kinsky, G., *A History of Music in Pictures*, New York, 1930.

LaRue, Jan, ed., *Aspects of Medieval and Renaissance Music*, New York, 1966.

Lowinsky, Edward E., Introduction, *Canti B* (Venice, 1502), ed. Helen Hewitt, Chicago, 1967.

———, ed., *The Medici Codex of 1518*, Monuments of Renaissance Music, III, Chicago, 1968, pp. 90–108.

———, Foreword, *Musica nova* (Venice, 1540), ed. H. Colin Slim, Monuments of Renaissance Music, I, Chicago, 1964.

———, "Music in the Culture of the Renaissance," *Journal of the History of Ideas*, XV (1954), 509 ff.

———, "The Function of Conflicting Signatures in Early Polyphonic Music," *Musical Quarterly*, XXXI (1945), 227 ff.

Ortiz, Diego, *Tratado de glosas sobre clausulas y otros géneros de puntos en la música de violones* (Rome, 1553), Kassel, 1936.

Reese, Gustave, *Music in the Renaissance*, rev. ed., New York, 1959.

Sachs, Curt, *The History of Musical Instruments*, New York, 1940.

Strunk, Oliver, *Source Readings in Music History*, New York, 1950.

Wangermée, Robert, *Flemish Music and Society in the Fifteenth and Sixteenth Centuries*, English version by Robert Erich Wolf, New York, 1968. (Contains many art reproductions.)

Index by Performing Ensemble

(Numerals indicate the number of the piece.)